GOD

A HANDBOOK FOR THE DISBELIEVER

Other Books by Gordon Massman

Shocks

The Essential Numbers

Core Sample

0.174: The Complete Numbers Cycle

Love

Death

Poem for a Dog

God

A Handbook for the Disbeliever

Gordon Massman

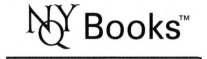

The New York Quarterly Foundation, Inc.
New York, New York

NYQ Books™ is an imprint of The New York Quarterly Foundation, Inc.

The New York Quarterly Foundation, Inc.
P. O. Box 2015
Old Chelsea Station
New York, NY 10113

www.nyq.org

First Edition

Set in New Baskerville

Layout by Raymond P. Hammond

Cover Design by Raymond P. Hammond

Cover Art: "St. Peter's in Rome: Explosion of Mystical Faith;" used with permission
© Salvador Dalí, Fundació Gala-Salvador Dalí, Artists Rights Society (ARS), New York 2017

Cover Art Source: Fundació Gala-Salvador Dalí

Author Photo by Shari Katz

Library of Congress Control Number: 2017947377

ISBN: 978-1-63045-033-5

God

A Handbook for the Disbeliever

For Bob Persing and Jim Feeley

I.

On Frenchboro's Island's eastern hell shore we discover
sticking through rotting hide vertebra curled in the
shape of it—tapered gargantuan spine—rostrum like
split inner tube, flukes ghosting off median notch,
black brittle skin baking on platter of fly-infested
kelp, vine upon putrid vine strung over rock like
stretched corpse-mask ringed by tide pools blistering
in sun. "Sacred," I pronounce repelling impulse to
haul home, display in yard beside derelict dingy,
concrete birdbath its grandest skeletal saddle. "This
is God, we must not defile." Patricia concurs. Nausea
from stink bilges up throat. This on our pristine
paradisiacal isle. "Xerxes!" I shout turning to go
as our Bull Mastiff whips chunks out God's side.

II.

God's in our mud, he's dead in muck, He inhaled
mud river, has become mud, His crown sunk, His
groin gashed by schist bleeds—red paint emptying
into black flood—He rock-struck skull, drowned,
one spies His hump, His starry hump, poor vapid
clown in our clump and swamp, vile thick down-
sucking stew, worm-beautiful—God lost in pitch,
mulch, sponge, muck, what impelled him here—
delusion? drug? despair? suicide? He might have
stayed in that fabulous lodge satisfied with His
whitefish, pork pie, library, smoking lounge,
might have ripened there, but something in
swampy mud beckoned like mother, whore—
damn all women their muddy hole—luring Him
to demise. Imagine the detestable flow down
throat, methodical python filling lungs, torso,
colon, gut, like poured cement, dead is dead,
but dead in crawling mud is doubly dead, and
I without ounce of breath or grace with which
to resuscitate hapless dunce, like spoon in vat
let him sink to bottom silt, to diarrheic substrate
and fossilize like trilobite, inscrutable rune of
ribs, ridges, unique massive geologic exhibit
to which bewildered seekers make continuous
pilgrimage, our adorable hapless mud-buried son.

III.

Mudslide buries children, mountainside relaxes
liquid slab over playground, muck-booted rescuers
extract corpses, mouths frozen in gleeful shout, eyes
open, all dead, foreshortened, but one…gurgling…
appearing to writhe…maybe…yes!…one giving
focus, hope…responders rush…boy! boy still
twitching!…against wall, alone, not in open…not
kickball or tag…in corner alcove…miracle boy!…
one lucky non-catastrophe family…standing by…
not wailing…here he is! mud-birth, blood-coated,
placenta-streaked…doctor-delivered…toes,
legs, shoulders, crown! crown! crown! upside-
down in rubber gloves, curled…naked, one shoe…
plastic ring…scrape face, blow lungs, clear
nostrils…rags, water, ambulance, tubes, triage,
triage…siren…one positive sub-headline: *Miracle
Child Survives Deadly Slide,* ministering hands
inside wagon, working, working, experienced
hands, oxygen glucose…head-to-toe scrub boy,
swab ears, navel, rinse hair, want hospital to
receive glowing child, Radiant One…BUT, medic!
quick!…what's?! something's?!…pound! slap!
shock! our savior, justification (rattling truck
screaming through traffic bearing stillborn God).

IV.

In brilliant tactical strategy
Jesus bumps in on donkey.
God is creative director for Ogilvy Mather.
He wears rags. Reverse snobbery.
Masses love it.
In favor of prayer He withers fig tree.
Riling multinationals He expunges capitalists.
Removes smut, He commands.
Tenderizes resistors.
Pries off lid.
Jesus has pitch: individual empowerment!
He dispenses tickets.
The entrenched want him dead.
He wants them whipped.
They are hucksters. He is Truth.
Time to rumble.
Jesus's heart's a switch blade.
Panther claw
Dripping blood of fury.
Clash of titans.
The captains close in, noose-tigthen.
God says Righteousness, Market Saturation.
Pounds it home.
The power elite says let him have supper.
Crackers and wine.
He's dead man.
Daddy says, it's decreed.
Nonviolent resistance.
It's in the copy.
But Daddy! Jesus off in some courtyard cries.
You can't mean...
Surely you don't...
Daddy sends him a tootsie pop.
Are you out of your...
Spit splats face.
Thong cuts flesh.
His bowels relax.
Snake of defilement.
Everything's fucked.
Airplane banner reads, *I'm Lovin' It*
Ponty Jr. pops candy corn.
What a massacre: whip, thorn, projectile, jeer, catcall, beam,

hammer, spike, shriveled Scrotum, vinegar, mock inscription
Against the ineffectual: *My kingdom is not of this world.*
Exit pretender.
Dead meat on stick,
Squirrel, possum.
Effeminate son embarrasses Father.
Abominations ensue.
Drunkenness. Nakedness. Sadomasochism. Pederasty. Sodomy. Slaughtered ox.
Labia And shaft
While lunatic bleeds rivers in the dark.

V.

God is male with big Priapus
God loves porterhouse steak
God mounts Mt. Massive
God runs steeplechase
God captains lobster boat, swallows snapping claws
God grease paints face, fires M134
God warbles women, closes for kill
God speaks Swahili
God ate his pudenda
God slept in mud flat, awoke inside baby's thumb
God dances flamenco with Heinrich Himmler
God eats nose gumdrop
God parades in bikini panties
God French kisses mirror
God licks mouth of kicked off stilettos
God loathes himself
God wants brains to blow out
God hates vaginas
God despises his list of despicable
God loves French demitasse
God collects Gregorian vases
God rockets to Thor's Helmet, back, out again, like Roger Rabbit
God wolfs double cheeseburger, fries, shake
God chews cuticles
God plays Putt-Putt with Roald Amundsen
God likes electric eels
God pumps tin carousel, hides face, counts to ten
God plugs ears with cinnamon sticks
God sulks after losing Trivial Pursuits to Foghorn Leghorn
God draws finger across nose after sticking it in ass
God does hokey pokey
God sets his hair afire, smothers it with DDT
God stuffs red apple in cheek, poses as baby
God eats Trident missile, burps
God can't stop laughing at men's pants
God worships carbon arrows
God jams navigational system, jets fly into ground
God climbs tree, howls
God fucks wolf in Chugach Range, prowls for mouton
God soaks tea bag in boar blood, paints tongue
God pumps semen through as many penises as women in creation
God octopus, squid, medusa, ball of snakes

God strings Bravo Company like popcorn, drapes it on tree

God suffers breakdown—guilt, shame, panic, insomnia—drags mattress into basement, moans at wife through floorboards, murders son, fist-pummels thighs, Upjohn, Pfizer, rigidifies into self-made prison, fixates on body—bowels, bladder, fat—writes poems on raw liver, checks into psyche ward, gets roommate with God delusion

God's mothers meet at Cheese Factory, decide on Camp Winnipesaukee

God packs bull whip, nudie magazines, Vaseline

God wants acquaintance with human viscera, becomes gastroenterological surgeon— unhappily— then goes to war

From Zippo tank God throws flame at motherfuckers

Let's not talk about it

Let's enjoy ice cream

God munching onion sandwich like curmudgeon curses propaganda, weather, slavish conformity, universal stupidity

God blows bubbles through soapy rag

God sucks t-shirt neck

God fails trig, graduates on technicality, in morning drags home reeking, half dead after night of dry humping

God, sick of circuses, festivals, victory parades, longs for death.

God, clapped into Bugatti Veyron, steps on it muttering "so long suckers", stops at zoo to look at monkeys

God dashes 100 dash backward to wave bye-bye to Usain Bolt

When Mary died God shaved head, self-flagellated, impaled heels, ate one hundred slugs full of slime, danced the mashed potato

God pops and chews glass tumbler, spits out the Milky Way

God slips on breezy after-marathon T, builds PPJ, sofa-reclines in ratty Minnetonkas, watches *Hunger Hiccups*

Barnum's Hall of Curiosities and Oddities features God's brother's sclerotic liver

God the Hypergraphic turns corner, smashes into God the Renunciate

Here is riddle: three men encounter bum dying in corner, one spits on "lazy bastard," one praising Darwin strides over him, one gives him cheese. Which is God?

God reads twelve novels, all wonderful but one, which is box of bees

God wants triplets, has twins, both die

Rat says God numbers my hairs, poet says God writes my poems, assassin says God blows my bomb, butcher says God's subdominant beast. God imagines a world full of fleas and kings but delivers a proletariat

On seventh minute of seventh hour of seventh day God poured Lime Rickey, got naked, pronounced all delightful, settled into the steaming green hot tub of the world.

VI.

In an unexpectedly nasal tone,
Finally, God speaks to me.
"Go to hell," he says,
Who do you think you're kidding
With your intellectualism, your
Dialectic materialism.
Bonehead. Buffoon.
With erector set,
Tonka truck.
God wizzles nose,
into handkerchief.
"Look at this,
Mr. Big Shot Cultural Studies Professor,"
And rams truck through cyclist.
Not odiferous palpable flesh,
But cold clammy cavernous breath,
Neither mellifluous nor hideous.
I would postulate I am dreaming
Were I not physically bleeding.
"Do you think, puny lizard
You possess transcendent wisdom—
Pitiable miniscule slitherer–
I could pop your eyes like blisters.
Let's go see Hell, he says
And flings me unmercifully
Into my own psychology.

VII.

Kids gather in cottage blistering
Under sun. One kid bosses.
They confer, scrawl figures:
Bizarre relationships
Of non-sexual nature
Only they, uniquely bonded, comprehend.
Something piratical, subversive,
Monumental
In clubhouse devoid of authority.
Unimaginable power!
Pubertal omnipotence!
Behind them into infinite distances
Rise mountainous commodiousness—
Animals, plants, minerals, fire
To bend to god-like fantasies
By kids
Sand-grit small, microscopically infinitesimal,
Insignificant.
One ejaculates: Yes! Absolutely!
Another with violent flourish annihilates optimism.
Another says, "Gentlemen, see here....!
None heed the tiny external squeak, "sandwiches!"
None crave lemonade.
One takes leak in enormous toilet. Incompletely washes.

The diagram! The equation!
The anointed formula!
(Not sexual, concupiscent.)
Oddly thick vaults,
For such inchoate organisms
Contain intense exhilaration.
One wears scarlet khaki shorts,
Another aqua cotton blouse,
Another, inexplicably, necktie.
Fourth seems almost naked.
One, disobediently, drags cigarette.
Another, equally Satanic, produces vodka.
This post of outlaws, secreted,
Oblivious and yet
Insularly crucial, and
As if through magical incantation, produce God.
One shouts: "Huzza, we are there!

Another: "Colleagues! Friends!"
Another: "There it is!"
And as they all sing
The sacred nursery rhyme
A massive fireball incinerates thousands.

VIII.

God listens to polite conversation of idiots and
is pleased, for all conversation, he knows, is
idiotic, even that of the philosophical professoriate.
The moral relativist smokes Luckies while
rational empiricist twirls vodka neat. Glorified
baboon novelist beds women on faux sensitivity.
God in palm cradles every fornication. See the
Joycean scholar at MLA delivering paper on
homoeroticism in Finnegan's Wake. God
enters veins like reverse-bacteria cleaning
blood with happiness. (Archivists will document
histories of the stricken.) Let us examine
family at breakfast: father punching yolk
with toast warns son on repercussion of
blowing math; mother stabbed by morning
sun, excoriates daughter's unkempt hair; Father
crushed by financial woe plots entrepreneurial
folderol. God shoots offspring to school,
father to work, mother to bed with migraine
headache. It is for God pathos, history.
Whose Fleece is white as snow….sending
up to Him inspirational prayer…his ignorant
bleaters. Well, He sighs, resigned, they
are, it's true, doomed. Sister weeps brother's
death rattle. At mother's fish-puffs son
claws air. Moved, God swaddles grievers
who gobble tears in therapy room. "He's so
critical." God enfolds her like broken wren.
"There, there." Really, it's like this. Suffering
molecular flood breaching dam, God sleep-
less internist succoring man. One drinks,
weeps. God cuts out collective human
tongue causing guttural echoes, ravaged
song, the hell of our own infinite brilliance.

IX.

Two orbs of brain at transducer tips encased in bone, dazzling.
Thank God for this machine.
Thank God for Coumadin.
Thank God females make eggs.
Vestigial tail cushioned by rump.
Thank God for these things.
Thank God for Cutters.
Thank God for ice maker.
Blood cleaning factory urethra-eliminating chloride, potassium, sodium, creatinine,
Thank God for grape sucker.
Thank God for Cling.
Thank God free shipping.
Hard palate separating food from nasal passage
Thank God for these numbers.
Thank God for fetal Doppler.
Thank God for seedless.
Vestibular, somatosensory, visual adduce to minimum postural sway against perturbation.
Thank God these wonderful thingamabobs.
Thank God Gorilla Glue.
Thank God I found it!
Nerves, alveoli, ganglia, papillary, cilia, glottis.
Thank God for indispensable kitchen devices.
Thank God for Flomax.
Praise God I lived!
The bloody thing works—digestion, efficiency, cognition, excretion.
Creates vaccine, isotope, microchip, rocketry.
Incomprehension paralyzes me.

X.

Politician, break at knees for victory.
Pray to constituent participation.

Realtor, petition for closing agent.
Supplicate before robust economy.

Novelist, implore for publisher.
Scrape before faceless bastion.

Salesman, entreat for gullibility.
Importune for salivating clientele.

Litigator, plead for catastrophe.
Solicit for tenacious protagonist.

Physician, prostrate to mutation.
Imprecate for rampant transmission.

Pastor, exhort for bankruptcy.
Genuflect to burnt heart-socket.

Prostitute, cry for scarcity.
Bow to emission desperation.

Fisherman, invoke for billfish.
Humble before slimy boat-gore.

Swindler, bow before naiveté.
Supplicate to trusting divinity.

Poet, obtest to Calliope.
Tithe for divine immolation.

Dictator, genuflect before rabidity.
Mortify to hypodermic patriotism.

All nighttime bedside kneel.
Plead for personal insemination.

XI.

People attend church, speak to God.

One entreats for prosperity,

"Please intercede with crucial negotiation.
This is life, well-being, survival…
All depends…must not fail…
Go insane…you owe…been good…
Would obliterate …everything stake…
Oh, God. Amen."

One entreats for forgiveness,

Reinstate me to centrality…weakened…19 years…
Never once…unthinkable… I descended…flesh…
Like drug…couldn't control…nobody's
Flawless…restore her to me…never
Again…ruined…shrivel up…amen.

One entreats for diagnosis,

Father, Protector, Savior,
Just this once…please, implore…for what is just…
Selfless…compassionate…sacrificial…
Be merciful…
"Nothing"… "benign"… "scar tissue"…
Spare…rebirth…glorious…amen.

One begs for fertility,

Dear God, Benevolent One…
Impregnate…fill me…his increase…
His platinum…atomic mushroom…in me…
Make me his honeybunch…heart swell…
His precious daisy…new life placenta-streaked…mine…ours…
Help me gratify…Amen.

One questions arbitrary survival,

Why me...critical...combative...imperious...
Depressive...and not he?...dear Lord...fore-
Shortened...children deprived of...am I then
Fated...destined...exemplar of Your solid
Qualification... didactic, disciplined, dicta-
Torial, cold...I give you...my solemn...to
Uphold...My sagacious One, Oh
Thank you thank you thank you.

One intercedes for humanity,

Heart that sees, marrow that knows...cornucopia...all
Everywhere simultaneously...plowshares...weep...
Blush with sorrow...what is?...where am?...what
Halcyon....lamb with lion...sweet arcadia...
Rivers of cream...paradise returned....
Love thy...cradle thy...abatement finally
Of cold hard sin...sunbeams...Hallelujah!

One lies

One confesses lies

One accuses

One cries

One fears suicide

One resolves...promises

One bargains

Pregnant with Thee is surfeit, sanctuary, ecstasy.

XII.

God enters Gordon like convict woods after escaping
crashed transport bus. Gordon's branches engulf him.
God wades bog, camouflages face with mud, eats
frog, bog weed. God needs gun, money, wheels; God
needs new mug. Gordon shelters under eggy moon,
Gordon accommodates. God blackens self under
brambles. Cops track with dogs. God's handcuffs cut
wrists. Damn things. God self-castigates: idiot, block-
head, blunderer. Gordon wraps night round God
like raw bacon. Hyper-vigilantly God sleeps, dreams
of Camp Winnipesaukee. God fantasizes Sylvester
Stallone. Blood shatters out Gordon's ears from
God's inhabitance. Acid flames throat. God feels to
Gordon like male goat. Damn it all. God's dirty. God
spits grit. God defecates magma. God's blood
impregnates mosquitoes. Gordon prays, "Stop this
pain, help me giggle." Gordon screeches like tea
kettle. Fugitive! Fugitive! Murderer! God penetrates
Gordon's pelvic swamp—bladderwort, skunk cabbage,
moccasin. David Livingston. God curls under pitch
pine, chews chick-weed root. Dozes. Authorities rake
purling mass but God slips through. Three years pass.
Rubble crushes Haitian babies. Indonesia boils in
tsunami stew. Sludge fills Peruvian schools. Gordon's
mother's flesh rots. Gordon abstracts. God thickens
like marbling clot. Gordon coughs out God like hair.

XIII.

Dear god, I am good. I have neither lied nor deceived. I
am honorable, faithful. I love only one, never waver. I
am clever, steady. I have cultivated art, am charitable. I
am pleasant, exude optimism. I love my children, am
devoted dad. I support them, engender self-esteem,
they repay me in kindness. I am temperate, sober, level-
headed, do not smoke, do not gorge sugar. I am strong,
energetic, work like mule. One will not discover me
loitering. I am self-motivated, tenacious at desk,
even in knowledge of mediocrity. I am rowing, always
rowing, enduringly. I loved my parents who expired in
my arms. I weep for suffering of humankind. Empathy
walks with me. I am kind to animals without whose
presence I would suffer. I am incapable of envy—those
ultra-talented, or jealousy—those who betray me
for rival. I am magnanimous, unable to possess by
duress: the un-caged bird. Ostentation repulses me. I
am more mendicant than prig. Humble in imperfection,
tummy sags, I am non-titanic. Comprehending futility,
I struggle not against my limitation, neither grand
nor heroic. Few will remember me after death. The
man writing this is parsimonious, pleased with left-
overs, Goodwill pants. I heal none. Emotionally, I have
cast off everything, am free, nothing is me. I am
naked on blank disk, courageous. One must, I accept,
biologically expire. I am already dead. I know one
must die daily to live fully. All things depart my hand
as dust. Dear God, take me when ready. I am unafraid.
Until then I shall be grateful for my life, and smile.

XIV.

God creates casino in Death Valley, twinkling firmament
motif called *Milky Way.* Constellations glitter on ceiling
like diamonds, comets streak, riches confront customer.
Gleaming cars rotate on mirrors. Exterior is nondescript
adobe, pink, windowless; blinking neon stars entice
traveler. Parking lot is dull black tray, but within brain
circuitry orgasms, clanging blares euphoria-jackpot.
Prostitutes mingle like heroine needles. Patrons select
scampi, porterhouse, Newburg, Kiev from *The Sanctuary*
buffet. Entertainers impersonate preachers in cavernous
auditorium. The compound includes *The Universe,* a
fascinating mirrored high-rise hotel where fucking
and suicides occur. In lavish suite overlooking floor
God keeps pistol, bodyguard, bank vault, whore. Pilot
dozes in chopper on roof. God loves his emporium,
they hail from everywhere—the innocents—inspired
by despair, would kill insurrectionist with antagonistic
zeal. Let species devour its own. And thunderous
clanging lifts, whirls winners sparkling through air,
places them down charismatic among the transfixed.
These spread the word and the word is…Euphoria!

XV.

God breaks sound barrier, achieves light
speed, then exceeds that, punching through
infinitely outstretching infinite universes
at increasing acceleration galvanizing all
into one quavering singing thread which
flashes indescribable enlightenment—
selflessness, purity wonderment, love—
into Jesus Christ of Nazareth's holy spirit.
I'm scratching a fly bite on my crack
while pondering a nasty weed infestation.

XVI.

Lord I forgive you your trespass, indiscretion, depravity, addiction,
I forgive everything. From henceforth let us proceed, friends in
ecstasy. I restore roundness, your unwounded state. I am
forgiveness. I, light. You need no longer bury head in shame.
I give you your world in original blossom, fresh readiness. Step
forward. I empower you to appear. Look at your thigh: healed!
your chest laceration: disappeared! Through me you are fresh.
This my gift, to join vigor with speed, speed to vigor. Like power
blowing life into clay, I command you to rule, your creation
awaits. King. Lord. Imbuement. God. You were lecher, liar,
swindler, thief. I blow you out like egg through shell, refill you
with bliss. My work is complete. Lord, it is yours. I give you
chlorophyll. Should you regress to your invidious behavior I
shall with one smite smash you through back of oblivion,
through pre-oblivion's cosmic dust, through that measureless
colorless etherized void to the sepulchral vacuum of death-
before-death where menace and idiocy cannot attach to
cytoplast and you are a billion billion light years from ignition.

XVII.

God raises Lazarus,
I wiz on dandelion.
God walks on sea,
I do the Egyptian.
God creates life,
I slice beef tongue.
God dies for sins,
I scratch fly bite.
God shows me
A thing or two:
Increases garden,
Empurples sky,
I pick head scab.
God gets serious:
Heals blindness,
Cures leper,
I clip nose hair.
God slaps me.
Nihilistically, I giggle.
God speckles night,
I eat Nut Roll.
God conducts bird symphony,
I treat genital wart.
God achieves mitosis,
I mumble Crow's Theology.
God creates *le petit mort.*
I pick teeth.
God says asshole,
I beat meat.
God says apocalypse,
I inflate vocal sac.
God says adios, motherfucker.
Slug slime,
Butt fuck,
Piece of shit.
Down jagged asphalt I drag
Flawless deformity.

XVIII.

God rents beach house, unpacks, monumental light,
sandwiches, station wagon, rubber raft. God sips
scotch bourbon while watching collegiate football.
He is married, going broke. He loves dramatic surf,
seafood: snapper, blackened trout. Thick sultry air
swells his cock which flops like ship rope. His two
young offspring of opposite genders migrate through
rooms like fatuous siroccos humming Bobby
Vinton. Early fifties just past Hiroshima. God's
best friend has rented adjacent Hutment, things are
hot, sloppy—humidity, heat, grit, mosquitoes.
God is undetectably desperate for money-bump,
He boat-fishes with buddy in glittering slough, rips
treble out croaking throat. Shot weight, swivel.
Flicks wrist, pops cork. God's wife, children, buddy,
His children swim in hot froth, saltwater washing
mouth. Rise, fall in sensual undulation, toes leaving
ground. This is love, paradise. Diamond ring
glitters. Youth. Creamy thighs. Slender hips. Lips
like couch pillows. L & M cigarette. Self-destructive
ideations slice God's brain camouflaged by bravado.
Nobody suspects. Frontal lobe conceals inwardly
cocked pistol. God slurps claw meat through hot
drawn butter, swigs Jax, brags—one table among
many. God's frog son zaps butter pat. We showed
those Japs. American ingenuity. And yet…How?
Where? Moans "Jesus Christ" in bait stand lava-
tory. Children have blast. God's wife despises him.

XIX.

Mouse's god is warm engine block.
God is lion's gashed zebra.
Millipede worships clammy clay.
Maggot hosannas guts.
Lice unburdens in pubic hair.
Tic sucks doxology dog.
Spit transports streptococci.
Aphid drinks blood of lamb sap.
What do locusts worship? Wheat.
Eagle snatches shad-Eucharist.
Skunk prays to chicken gizzard.
God is weevil's holy boll.
Let there be light.
Let there be love.
Seahorse lays eggs in God.
Krill ball inspirits whale.
Fruit fly hymns rotting pear.
Yea, though I walk.
Spider is scorpion's host.
Rat is psalm to cat.
Pedophiliac kneels to toes.
Sugar, starch bacterium exalt.
Bee's divinity, queen.
Mollusk chants sting ray,
Vulva, says bull.
Only I know God's identity
Shouts toad: boy.
Mama, intuits boy.
I resurrection, life.
Tug to fisherman.
War is God says bomb.
Fools! Fools! Love's God,
Shouts Bliss.
Bosh, blasts Bitter.
Cynicism's Spirit.
I am God pounds God,
(Flatware rattles,
All rivet.)
Intolerant, cruel.
Twit! retorts atheist,
Logic rules.
Logic's indomitable.

Tycoon: money's immutable.
Enthrone me, enthrone me,
Madhouse rumbles.
Squirted free, outside,
Above the fray,
Only dancer dancing
Embraces God,
Haughtily.

 **XX.**

I ejaculate God. God is half billion magmatic fish
flowing over fist. I touch his fluffiness. Lover on
knees swallows God like Eucharist. My kitchen floor
is Catholic church. Holy scripture falls open on
blank pages, as does Jane Eyre, Moby-Dick. God
inhabits no book, purse, nor musical note. He is
come comfortably. I love God, shoot him constantly,
hand frenzied whip, bleed under circumcision lip,
am only happy when he's pooled unformed child
to whom I pray, for whom I ache. Like reptile I
crawl on breasts spilled with God. I finger paint
face. God is quick and sometimes cruelly cheap
when worshipped alone. I haven't thought it through.
When I die one, merely, of God's gushers dies.

XXI.

I title this poem *God*.
God is appropriate
Because this poem identifies
And defines God.
I thought weightily about titles.
I rejected *Who Art in Heaven*
For cutesiness.
I discarded *In Whom We Trust*
For nationalism.
I purged *Credo in Deum Patrem omnipotentem*
For pretentiousness.
I refused numerous ecumenical
Denominational doxological
Clichés
Involving beneficence, munificence, omniscience, benevolence.
Finally, only *God,* suffices
For this poem
Visualizes, demystifies, alphabetizes
The unintelligible and unknowable
For all to see.
I begin it now.

XXII.

Elvis is God.
No Dionne Warwick is God.
Oppenheimer, for sure.
Hell no, Michelangelo.
Shakespeare, dammit. Willie Shakespeare.
BS. Eric Clapton.
Eric Who? Give me break. Hendrix.
Marilyn Monroe is God, end of story.
Lincoln is God, always was, always will be.
Bach, God dammit. JS Bach.
King, you boob, Martin Luther King.
Sure King is something, but Duke Kahanamoku, QED.
Wrong Duke, buster, Ellington, Duke Ellington.
You mean Jim Morrison.
Like hell, I mean Duke.
Morrison had it all over Duke.
Betty Boop!
Gary Cooper!
Larry Csonka!
Who are you kidding: Ingmar Bergman, Period. Exclamation point!
Jose Feliciano.
What, that charlatan? Mr. Ed is God.
Oh sure, Hitler is God. You've got to give him that.
Forty-two million's nothing to sneeze at.
I am God says Avery.
I am God says Meghan.
I am God says Dean.
Oreo cookie is God. Double Stuff.
Yea, like Lorna Doone, numbskull. Cocaine is God, Everybody knows that.
Levi jeans is God. Levis, indubitably.
You're all batty: sex is God.
Yea, sure, genital slop zone is God. What joke.
Einstein is God.
Freud is God.
Crawling out ground zero cockroach is God. Nothing other.
Death is God, nothing beats death.
Jesus did, ninny.
Poppycock!
Jesus!
Baloney!
Of Nazareth!
Balderdash! Claptrap! Hog wash! Hooey!

Sleep, I say, unconsciousness.
Andy Warhol, incontestably. Campbell soup can.
For all you nincompoops, to settle this once and for all,
Coco-Cola is God, pure and simple:
Omnipresent. Omnipotent. Omniscient. Omnibenevolent.

 XXIII.

I created God in my image. Also, every human birth
replicates me, every death a piece of myself returned
to me, reusable. Human is my masterpiece equipped
with ingenuity, self-awareness, creativity. Beasts I
made counterpoint—simple, linear, single-minded.
I enjoy God but savor sapiens who strive for
sophistication. Some play music, some paint pictures,
others compose poetry. Dante, Beethoven, Buonarroti.
God impresses me less—laughable foppish twit.
In designing him I included everything. Turned
out insufferable. For him a distant cumulous.
But gooey my humans with their valentines, love-
sick croon, barked knuckles. Such darlings. I failed
to include maturation. Still, with their splitting pre-
dicaments they entertain where God is tiresome
sissy. I plan to annihilate God who corrodes human,
by gradual entropy or slow cancer—removal too
precipitous could crack collective human psyche.
My precious ones, I promise downy landing.
Make love. Have babies. Caress. Produce. Your
stability is my oxygen, your tears my suffocation.

XXIV.

God dashes about thicket like madman, resin-streaked,
rent shirt, peering through branches. One has to
love him, terrified of everything. I offer peanuts, he
disappears. I think he's wild-child animal raised,
spooked by everything. Denizen of grotto, comfortable
in chlorophyll, scooped den. Peering through
window at Chez Michel: glinting crystal, Pompano
en Papillote, God outside in sleet, baffled, like
sylph, vanishes. God tears raw skunk. One glimpses
him behind brake with what appears a flute.
Sea Dyaks of Borneo spot him devouring raw
shad. Hunting parties emerge empty-handed while
summits on theorems and scientifically approved
civilizing techniques abound. He is believed to
possess supernatural power. One hones data,
one cleans lenses, one invokes annals. Filing nails
I await, endlessly glancing. Governments possess
cages big enough for Mythopoesis. Man has
captured gargantuan creatures. But this chimerical
flicker, figment…I am lousy writer, dilettante.
God appears uncannily in family photographs,
Those reunion, anniversary, milestone exposures,
professionally composed on sloping lawn. Who
is that? Where did he come from? Who put him
there? In chair, eyes closed, head in hands I
induce dream state, psychic portal, fertile sub-
conscious atmosphere through which to receive
a visitation. Nothing appears, not even a shadow.

XXV.

I chop off God's head, he dashes about barnyard
spurting blood. I pluck, fry, devour Him. For
one day He imbues me with breath, like roman
candle pulse. Soon I eliminate waste. I call this
prayer. How much blood has earth absorbed?
My mother forgave me, died. My father died
blithering gibberish. I behead another chicken.

XXVI.

Rabbi Wolf infused with fire delivered benediction,
tallit-draped arms spread like heron wings. Fifty
years later I still feel scorched. Mother's coffin rests
beside his. He was terrifying, authoritative who
taught Hebrew, presided over Bar Mitzvah.
After confirmation I denounced religion, wedded
to anti-intellectualism. I worshipped women,
alcohol, literary fiction while Wolf faded like patina-
stained statue. What was Hebrew, Yad, tabernacle,
shofar to butch waxed big shot? Or sacred
Kaddish, *Yit'gadal v'yit' kadash sh'mei* to swaggering
know-it-all? Make me humble? Trap me in
convention? Impact superstition? This liberal
social democrat? Wolf, wringer washer, went
obsolete—ancient bird-beaked dictatorial antique
rotting beside mother. Give me Led Zeppelin.
Give me Hollywood. A lifetime ago great-grand-
mother buried in earth unclean dishes, employed
on Shabbat only shoes. Her daughter scooped
candle smoke over scarf-draped head. Her daughter,
my mother, lit occasional taper. I was atheist, re-
placing God with logic. But now future hardens
into impenetrable blank flat-matte wall from whose
pin-point center Wolf, sizzling, emerges, arms out-
spread, stentorian, alive, and not so contemptible.

XXVII.

God is saltine, when snapped particles fly
God is alligator's stomach, fangs
God is ancient human skull exhumed
God is reading Ruth Rendell during thunderstorm
God makes me sick
God induces dry heaves
God is dog thermometer
God is reading on LSD Gerard Manly Hopkins
God is psychopathic incapacity toward empathy
God is therefore genocidal
God is equally spermicidal
God mows down with machine gun
God murders to hosannas
God wins football championship, war, rodeo, grand prix
God jacks off to porn
God worships his irresistibility, cannot resist self
God is male, women; God is male
Stomps on things
God wears necklace of mirrors
God's middle finger diddles gaudy silver ring
God is love, forgiveness, munificence, fly swatter
God collects shavings from pencil sharpener barrel
God savors Sunday morning, Planet Earth, which showers him with inspirational   spit
God answers all petitions with universal grunt
God watches reality TV show in which departed souls descend into pit
God simply adores Kellogg's Special K soaked in goat milk
God loves ball popping mitt in crisp Boston Fall
God attends retrospective of Hieronymus Bosch, takes east exit laughing uproariously
Tyrannosaurus God angrily bursts from house, grabs two brawling kids by
    collar, knocks their heads together
God awakes, pees Amazon River, dribbles Lake Superior
God prays to God who prays to God who prays to God inside shark's belly
That's it, by golly, that's it!
I have it!
Infinite universes radiate infinitely within a single bubble in an infinity of bubbles
    exploding outward in every direction while simultaneously collapsing into the pupil
    of an eye's
Hollow deep swirling which is called God
God, I say, *God,* and responds the void, *No*
No? I say. Affirms, *No.*
No, no, no, no, no, no,   no
Not mist fog ether air atoms molecules nanoseconds minutes years decades love hate
loneliness bliss rage spectacles underwear geckos crickets lizards…No

Bees mass into ball, blot sun
Barnum's lion crackers detonate like bombs
I, suddenly crying
Everything destroyed
God wraps mouth round flame thrower, blows
Victory euphoria
Celebration orgy
God owns alley he weaves drunk
Dinner served: raspberry vinaigrette, candied yams, human liver, God's favorite
Rita Hayworth, Lana Turner, Merle Oberon, Carole Lombard
God is hammer, nail, board, structure, neighborhood, county, country,
    planet, galaxy, universe, infinities heaped upon infinities in ontological and
    phenomenological unintelligibility
I slice thumb on broken window
Relief! Screams gash, I apply wrapping. *Relief!* Screams hostage, ball joints
Strappado-cracking
Gerard Manly Hopkins blubbers theoretical
I am vengeance, transgressors shall know horror
Ye shall flay yourselves, shove flesh into each other
Ye shall frenzy in hellish waste
I cauterize heart, perforate you in Iron Maiden
They who open it discover pure virginity
Dawn here is dusk there, noon here midnight there, fresh here stale there, light at
0, dark at 180, scrape round the sphere, the old weep
God oh God oh God oh God
Ecstasy, dejection
Perish   perish perish perish parish/\/\/\/\
Let there be let there be…something blinding flashes horizon…in blast-wave
    buildings crumble…beauty, devastation swirled together fill eyes with
    multicolored liquid glitter humans cry.

XXIII.

Pity man his strutting braggadocio
Pity man his personal panacea
Pity him his compulsive calisthenics
Pity man his vocal apparatus
Pity painter his incomparable masterpiece—pigments, applicators
Pity the symphonic *piece de resistance* overwhelming senses
Pity bombs, missiles, magnificent detonations
Pity man his sexual instrument
Pity man his gorgeous roast beef
Pity us our enviable real estate
Pity man glorious armistice
Pity us our gay romantic dazzling cities
Pity us our lethal brilliant indispensable board rooms
Pity human arboretums
Pity human blockbuster superheroes
Pity Maserati aficionado
Pity riders of world's biggest roller coaster
Pity human his Heisenberg Principle of Uncertainty
Pity man riding atop solid fuel jet propulsion
Pity spectators screaming for Alice in Chains
Pity preeminent authority on epistemological luminosity
Pity intimates at dinner party in which mutual superiority is affirmed
Let us pity the inestimable dramatic thespian in Hollywood warehouse at pinnacle
    of power filming the most brilliant screenplay of the century
Let us pity, I say, famous editor at award ceremony
Gimme a T, Gimme an E, Gimme an X, Gimme an A, Gimme an N, Gimme an S.
        TEXANS! TEXANS! TEXANS!
Pity man all-time best in world most incredible favorite animal
Pity human his heavyweight clean and jerk champion of world
Let us, then, pity, finally, insurrectionists storming presidential mansion
Pity man his Ulysse Nardin Genghis Khan Grand Complication Minute Repeater
Tourbillon 780-88
Pity man swaggering down Madison Avenue after closing deal of lifetime
Pity humans their fabulous addictions
One pities man standing behind six foot wide bank check stunned by camera after
    winning publisher's clearinghouse sweepstakes
Pity young Neptune who wins gold, scores lucrative contract with General Mills
Let us mourn Steph and Gene whose baby just skidded to planet
Give us this day our daily, forgive us all, lead us not
Pity rock star jacking off with Stratocaster to cheering
Pity poor William, Chief otolaryngology surgeon at St. Luke's Presbyterian
    handsomely rewarded, cherished, exalted

Pity poor human ejaculating under insulated attic, moonlight pouring through window

Pity founder of Federal Electronic Retrieval Corporation, wealthy beyond imagining, yachting to Grenadines

Pity Carrington, Hollingsworth, Willoughby, Covington

Let us retrieve from abyss of misery two Supreme Court justices, three Ballerinas, four baseball sluggers, five heads of state, six Nobel Laureates, seven venerated generals, eight contemporary novelists, nine Catholic cardinals, ten sudden celebrities, a fireman and a brewery king.

Let us pity lovers whose kiss explodes like rocks smashing surf

Let us pity, then, remorselessly—steam hissing seam—the accused the instant courtroom bursts into relief at words "not guilty"

That is all, must be all, there is God with which to contend, countless others present, equal, identical shuddering off ground in great froth of power, drunkenness, pride, eyes, hair, stride animated with money, sectioned off, dividing up, wobbling through space like blown soap bubbles, oblong, jolly, oval, more's pity, more's sorrow, more's charity, let us plead let us summon let us wail for cold cucumber salad plate, frosted sherbet punch bowl of salvation in rushes, for the luminous, profound, pervasive.

XXIX.

"Yeah, but what about natural beauty? What about that!
Oceans, butterflies, forests, gorges. Riddle me that.
Can you doubt God's existence and gaze upon sequoia
simultaneously? Have you seen Grand Canyon, Arizona?
When it comes to that how about Kilimanjaro?
And you beating your atheistic tom. There's more
God in one maple leaf than space in your Nothingness.
Put that in your pipe, Popeye. Do you not pray?
Do you not unburden? Do you not employ song
against suffering? Hummingbirds alone prove God's
infusion. Screw human ugliness: crime, war, addiction,
fornication: this is detritus of inferior species, arrogant
bug. Look to great blue heron, bullfrog for proof.
Not to mention infinities of universes spilled across
cosmos. Look to spider silk. You can take your
Ferrari, and Audemars Piguet and lunar space
toy and Sistine Chapel and trash them in dump,
grease-clots of idolatry. God is El Capitan, Galapagos
tortoise, that stubby phlegmatic sage, Cliffs of
Moher, the tiniest pea aphid in wood. All your
nuclear bombs can't annihilate that. You and
your empiricism. I had mother slap me across
face. Father flushed my head in john. I know
about man, I know about God. One finds God
beyond horizon of human skull. Marriage is idol.
Baby is idol. Happiness idol. Sanctuary idol.
Flea sipping droplet sparkling on leaf is God,"
He said. I thought how stunning that
Syllables can click together like sections of
a needle to pierce the heart with minimum
resistance for maximum easeful lethality,
more elegant that quantum mechanics,
theoretical mathematics. Yet teeming,
smoldering, hostile, dictatorial, bone-
headed, dumb-tongued, heart-stupid sea
of depravity lumbering down slab concrete.

XXX.

I'm unaffected, continue routine. I body sculpt
at club morning dog dies. I attend mother's
funeral, fly home, work. I'm counterbalanced.
I do not empathize with friend's lymphoma,
chug beer at Barnaby's Crab Shack. I split life
like ax: mine, theirs. Divorced today, clubbing
tonight, swig, flirt. Lovely towhead. Nothing
flusters. Steadiness. Through world straight black
line, Pilot Point. Porterhouse, medium rare,
fries, Catchup, Guinness. The Ticket: don't
get sucked into other's drama: loss, failure,
illness, fire. I'm independent kinesis. Light
surrounds my fingertips. My destiny smashes
highway turtle, unmoved. Screw turtle. I
use sharp pencil. Military doesn't emote,
military locks ambition, jaw muscle. Jackie
delivers baby, I'm marathon training. Day
she delivered, I jogged eight miles nail-
faced. (Baby owns her breast.) I need no
God, have none other than propellant self.
Eyes upon me, I vault into next century.

XXXI.

In masterstroke, Jesus becomes god
Bang! God. Resurrection! God.
Woman spreads word. God spoke.
Tell friends. Absolution is here. Abishag
Stumbles on rock. Citizenry
Fans out. Hills overspill. Sandals.
Staffs. Filthy husbandry. Quarry
Marble blocks, cedar sanctuary.
Tendrils grope. Men in purple
Wield great power, wealth.
Ride in Hupmobile. One owns
Maserati. Ant bed. Ant bed.
Hot granulated dirt. Savage
Slits one's throat. Another
Blows up hypocrites. War!
Brilliant white flash. Up crawls
Jesus from zero like roach,
Triangular, shiny, black
Which blossoms into space-
Age supercar before which
the grotesque congregate.
Eighteen hundred horses.
Aerodynamic. Faceted.
Through bomb dust it juts
Like quartz crystal. Its shaft
Slams through the heart.

XXXII.

Oh hell everything's so goddamn beautiful
botany zoology people everything natural
alive so bloody precious the cosmos light
dark twilight everything between sounds
barking talking howling screeching pitches
timbres and domiciles nests hives beds lairs
it re-solidifies stands him up stiff evokes
prayer good God almighty hallowed be thy
majestic works more alive than I've ever
dying dog chlorophyll seam weeping sister
split me down middle in revere jolting
blood dark sequin red full of brilliance
torque speed human Lamborghini ocean
waves swelling cresting smashing spearing
gulls flashing minnows silver night star-
smear ice cold whole bloody thing filling
gills with richest blood foil platinum
breathing flesh breathing one I'm solid
fuel and the contrasts emerald on gray
scarlet on green tan on slate stack upon
stack gradations of black and all those
infernal human movements surrealists
expressionists conceptualists tragi-comic
May Day parade sickle and womb sickle
and womb and how one aches with the
gut punch doubled in alley mussed un-
tucked buckled crying for God in the glit-
tering litter oh steady me buttress me I'm
nauseated with creation's oceanic over-
powering superabundant sumptuousness.

XXXIII.

God numbers hairs on your head
And hairs on every head
In world He numbers
And each newborn's hair gets numbered
And each death's hair gets subtracted
From total
And the accounting's frantic, continuous
With innumerable statisticians in cubicles
Throughout cosmos
For number of hairs is astronomical
And those which drain sucks down
Are equally included with exactitude
And God also numbers body hair—
Pubic, armpit, buttock—
Such that only God's calculator is big enough,
Bigger than Berkeley supercomputer,
Yet incomprehensively miniscule—
Subatomic, yet we know it exists
Under, as it were, God's fingernail.
Let it be crowed that God loves us
Beyond imagining
Protects from catastrophe
Each of us his hirsute flock
And each follicle matters even if shorn
And tipped into pan,
Such as traitor's neck hair shaved for guillotine,
The cleanest barbered back of neck may appear
Bald but in God's omni-penetrating gaze is not overlooked,
But woman plucking eyebrows diminishes her number,
And faces buried under beards and head hair
Have nothing on soldier in number
And, therefore, significance.
Hear ye, hear ye,
Nuclear physicist, symphonic composer
Are not superior to mendicant
In God's mind
So stop strutting.
And contradictorily the congenitally hairless—
The alopecia areata sufferer—
And the shiny-headed chemo patient have
As much reason to smile as
Dreadlocked Rastafarian

For hair though numbered is peripheral,
Metaphor
For God's inclusiveness,
God's unwavering benevolence,
I have heard, too, that God judges
Every thought in every head
In the world
But that's another story,
Incomprehensible.

XXXIV.

God said let there be darkness and there was darkness.
Light is world's original state. God split light with
sin for He was bored. He needed peep show to
grease masturbation. Adam, Eve numbed him with
tepidness. And so He created shame, naughtiness,
exhibitionism, addiction. Dripping spit. Pro-
nounced it right. Now delicious videos. Hot
XXX. Eve didn't give head. God hired world's
top hit man, half in advance, half on delivery,
who wound about trunk hissing cost-benefit.
Adventuresome, Eve bit. God drooled watching
shame-mixed sex, rubbed hands. God said less
light, more dark—lab mouse hitting bar—and
darkness fell like black crepe wherein sin—war,
rape, slavery, bacchanal—shot through world
like bloody thread. God slobbered, ate crazy
corn. Light like weed peeps through concrete,
God shoots it with Round-up. Let there be dark
and it was delicious with sex-laced violence,
spree killing, delectable AIDS, provocative
starvation. God's biggest hard-on is witnessing
still births: meaningless labor. You can't blame
owner of such efficient ax for splitting tedium
in half, light cleaved open. One loves spilled
viscera. Whose apogee is soldiers gang raping,
murdering girls before their mothers, then
slaughtering the mothers. This for God is a binge.

God has sex with Death; Death, submissive female, rolls on back.
She fucks God so blind his eyes glitter like planetarium. Joe
is hoodlum dispatched to hades. Death's vagina closes as God
withdraws penis. Revelation in coupling. Forevermore they
are inseparable, mutually vehement against intruders. Death
shops, God works. Death fries chops, God negotiates deals.
God is in love, slips home for quickie. Glows does God,
eternally. Hammer thrower. Death's beautiful as thousand
Cleopatras, zooming bosoms, jet black nest, toes like heroin.
God simply rages, desire snaps off back like fire. *Babycakes,
sugarplum,* God warbles, *honeybunch.* Death has taught
Achilles, winking ridges, downy freeways, she sweeps
like valley, but feels like silk pudding, enters God, spreads.
God cannot press all of her. Indomitable symbiosis: inde-
fatigable double suction. Gravity nails to whirling planet
tasty people Death, God pop amidst sex-a-thon. With
table grapes. Mortals have their little: love-rush, symphonic
composition, gyration ritual, war euphoria. Mortals have
their biscuits. But God fucks Death like solar system.
Danny prays for Midge. Midge prays for stasis. Peter prays
for yes. God's impaling Death deaf dumb blind. And
breaking apart after spasm both laugh at dead soldiers
littering their courtyard like offered morsels. Satiated,
Death scoops up mortals, serves them to God, depleted.

XXXVI.

THE GOD MONOLOGUES

1.

Take Georgette, for instance: strenuously petitions for benignity,
beseeches parenthetically for Bengali urchins, "forsaken
angels." Pleads for negative oncological report. Quivers,
essentially. I am merciful, omnibenevolent, desire reprieve,
but Georgette muddies by rude contradiction. I know
her heart—envious, avaricious, conniving bitch, mortally
materialistic, clandestinely unsympathetic, empathy soiled
by black narcissism. Not simple case. One of my most
physically arresting creations, creamy skin, delicate bones,
small perked breasts, Cupid lips, "drop dead" as humans
say, heroin to men. She loves hard pumping. Intensely
tortured. Guiltily, she betrays, achingly repents. Emotionally
inaccessible. Do I rescue in munificence this disingenuous
creature? I possess no checklist. Gradations are everything.
I'm leaning toward death—nasty thing fornicating with
athletic trainer, shoplifting lipstick (which I could strike
into rose bouquet!). But I am conflicted. This scorpion
stings while I consider. You who believe me implacable
master note this tender equivocation. Georgie's witty,
engaging, blessed with lust, stick of TNT not easily consigned
to premature extinction. Her child's interest prefigures,
too, though secretly not husband's increase. She's decent
to domestics. Do not imagine, interloper, that with your
vicarious idle interest you shall witness my proclamation.
That moment belongs to her alone, but know that between
now and this final decision your callous Ruler suffers.

2.

Like you each morning I dress—woven tie, tweed coat,
chino slacks—down Krispies, fire ignition. Like you I fret—
failure, inadequacy, dismissal, ridicule. Like you I suffer
compulsions, mine involves consecutive numbers. Like
you I detest my job; existence, in fact. Unlike you I have
no God. Like you I'm hooked, sugar addiction. I despair
of constipation, acid reflux. Like you am weary of biological
function, would rather be automaton. Like you I fear
extinction, yours material, mine spiritual, strive toward
continuousness. Like you necrotic, rotted in places. You
think me incorruptible permanent fixture. Like you I
get dirty requiring soap. I emit bestiality—armpit odor,
gritty sweat, fecal stink. Like you I want soaking. Oh,
I am lonely, too, heart a far-flung nebulae. Like you I
crave novelty—for you Corvette, for me new human
tragedy. Each night I loop keys on peg, unknot tie, pop
cork, sigh out stress like crinkling beach shingle. Like
you I revive, tease out bliss like basketful of snake. Last
night I dreamed tsunami stiffened by cracked sea bed
buried a village, scything people dashing for safety.
Gleeful playboy, I created that swell, whimsically. Killing
people cuts monotony. Imagine my ejaculatory howl—
my geyser ecstasy—as collapsing structures crush dozens.

3.

Heaven is dog sanctuary, if you're interested. If you're really
fascinated heaven is cacophonous pandemonium. Kibble, bits,
bits, kibble. Ironically, I'm perturbed that you, man, designed—
because it doesn't exist within your species—such vessels of
undivided loyalty. Poor unsuspecting creatures. Yet how
deny these blameless angels. Take Plato, for instance, starved
beside corpse of fallen master. I took Plato's soul unwaveringly.
Or dumped Blakely marched pads to pulp home to drunken
bastard. Need I further enumerate? Pit bull is innocent, and
shepherd dog-soldier not responsible for ideology, The place
is a multi-dimensional infinitely wide universe of dog parks.
I love them. Yesterday Spats, boy's companion, spun to me
like wind-blown paper. I, God, wept. Blighted is man, sadistic,
duplicitous, murderous lout. I created monsters, guiltily,
who invented gentle creatures in which to soothe blood-soaked
hands. Well, I don't inhabit Earth; besides I have grudgingly
accepted some human martyrs. Jesus compacted himself into
dog, muzzle to hock, dewclaw to tail, Bichon to Bouvier des
Flanders. Compare to your angry grudges, tawdry predilections,
trashy infidelity. Heaven would be blighted. If you want to
know with your chlorinated swimming pools, NASDAQ,
iPad, genocides heaven is dog paradise, if you really want to
know, scattered with the few miniscule humans crawling in
hedges, awestruck before the Rushmore of dog knuckles.

4.

Superstitiously you imagine me omniscient, omnipotent,
omnipresent, omnibenevolent when I am actually
crack-toothed malodorous opinionated house painter
sick of brushes who cannot die. My telephone blares
another job, Yachtsman Blue, Oceanic Green—some
delusional fool—and here I come with crusty ladder,
drop cloth, diabetic blood while Mr. Slick conquering
world tears off in Audi. Half blind cynic, I apply,
mutter, curse lousy bastard. I seal house with paint ,
flat matte finish, shield from severe neurological
weather for which you give me homegrown ears.
I don't ease to sleep but collapse like scaffold,
leathery skin, latex nails. Here's human's greatest
folly, the chasm between dream and reality, the
botanical bridge to Hell's casino. Orgasm Red,
Paradise Cream, Coconut Blue. Briefly I bought
hypodermic lie, carried like hero "shoulder high"
atop mob's frenzied victory but truth intruded in
vodka tumbler. I am mostly man, dissolute, dis-
eased, exhausted, angry, dangling tin mundane
pots. Give me thirsty wood to satisfy. My brushes
of prettiest hue disguise all manner of dissolution.

5.

You think I'm King of Kings? You think you're central,
core, You think on human lap I loll? Let me dis-
abuse. I never consider you. Rather be dead. I hear
your plea for courage, strength, for hospitalized
Judy. You beseech believing I see. Fool. You'll
contract cancer without intervention. I'm happy up
here with jigsaw puzzle. Weather's Jake. Lake's
sweet. Buzz off with your catastrophe. You miniscule
soft-bellied dirt-walkers, you think I'm yours with
your Eucharist. And that parable of the single foot-
print in sand, Gotta laugh. What egocentrism.
Your blathering religion, righteousness. Oh, I do
intermittently pity with your coitus, alcohol,
Pulitzer Prize. Die giggling. And ritualized tearful
funeral. Fragile thin-skinned mendicant. And
money: what brutality. Take my advice: embrace
star-smear, infinities heaped upon infinities like
soap bubble mansion. Take my advice: marry,
procreate, possess, celebrate, pretend you matter. I've
got sunset to catch on Cigar Galaxy. Sure, I empathize,
you're in French trench, death's popping skull-
skittles. Scared, you pray. You think I'm attentive.
Consider billions of petitions simultaneously gushing
out world's rooftops, syllable-inundation billion
miles thick and assess your significance. Nutball.
I'm hauling on shoulder dead stag I bow-killed
to slaughter for winter, I'm ax-splitting heartwood
for raging hearth fire, sharp palpable reality against
the simpering obsequious butler you think I am.

6.

Okay, you got me. I *can* be magnanimous. Though how you
recognized me, and in fiction section where serendipitously
I discovered Schwarz-Bart's **The Last of the Just.** There
shall be what you term "divine intervention": newborn
Consuela, Rhabdomyosarcoma. No, won't have it. Why
she? Arbitrary, dear man. In vicinity. What? You dislike
my outfit? Vulgar? Undignified? Sometimes it gets me,
right here. She'll recover inexplicably. Where surgeon
expects carcinoma, clean CAT scan. There'll be sore
knees in Paraguay. My dear, attrition is necessary. What
war doesn't handle, illness must. You can't expect—I
mean, such grandiosity. But haphazardly, yes, when I
visit your spheroid. You think I'm omnipresent, pah!
Occasionally I wander into hospital, and children,
only children. I can suffer myself. It's you who suffer
without me. And I'm material, as you see, not ethereal.
I resemble in fact, wouldn't you agree, Ernest Borgnine.
You must accept your aloneness, friendlessness. Yes,
you caught me in stereotypical biblical moment justi-
fying your mythology, healing terminal baby. Gloat.
Strut. High five a believer. Perhaps my physique revealed
me through this Patagonia regalia. I preferred anonymity
but got *People Magazine.* So be it. In your universal
social-psychological cesspool you need a little purity.
Consuela is healed. Celebrate her arrival as I vanish in air.

7.

This is quiz show. I'm Charlie Van Doren.
I know answers. Physics. Antiquity. Medicine. Philosophy.
I know everything ubiquitously. Anthropology.
I am three hundred thousand up.
With your TV cutlet watch me smack buzzer.
Michel de Montaigne!. Deoxyribose, two each purines, pyrimidines!
I astound. I mesmerize.
You see power I wield? You see what I am?
Challenge me; you won't win blender.
I'm cerebral blood.
Significance.
Wednesday night, eight o'clock, everyone transfixed.
Nabisco, General Electric.
See Cracker Jack. See Wiz Kid.
Question has not been posited that I cannot…
I knew solution before construction of riddle.
I pass through brilliance like chair
Through paint.
Phenomenal I'm.
Do you understand? Do you internalize?
Lightning wraps my crown.
My fingertip eclipses.
Pain-faced chorister issuing
Inspiration is zenith of absurdity,
Alcohol-clear emptiness engulfs melody
Quarter mile out
Like handful of thrown dust.
Lonely human in habitable envelope.
Bells clang. Board flashes. Jackpot!
Thunderbird convertible, ninety thousand smackers.
Can you keep secret? It's fixed.
Whole shebang.
Executives determined man needs illusion,
Hero,
Vicarious well-being.
You project me onto everything,
Microorganism to Milky Way.
I'm poor faker. With all my luminosity.
Privately, you know. Crude ubiquity exposes.
Of course I'm imaginary.
I'm you talking to yourself.

8.

I create stomach for amusement, most devilish invention.
For it, slave or starve. It gnashes until fed, gnashes again.
Vicious. Creation devouring itself. Wilderness of blood.
Slaughter factories—hooks, drains, bolt guns, concrete
holocaust, hands clasping pistol like baby rattle. Above all
I adore my stomachs, my twin duodenums. Emperor at
coliseum. Thumb down. Shark voracity. I grab toes, rock.
Greatest entertainment. Gnawing spine. Life-wasting
labor. Spoonful of soup. Temporary satiation. I'm spastic
with laughter. Hiccupping. Animal panic is my giddiness.
Anything. Anything. Prostitution. Gambling. Garbage
collection. Flooring it through city to crucial presentation.
Gasoline, parking lot. Wrapped around stomach Van
Allen belt of indifferent tenderness. He with satiated gut
is godfather. I observe smug or desperate faces kill lower
species, each other, gullet salivation. Makes me jolly, lethal
ballet of predation, terror on stage of such natural beauty.

9.

Roy Roger's scarf flipping in wind as Trigger gallops
forward through gunpowder smoke puffs, one, two,
three, Bullet leading charge, ears sleeked, then fist
fight, Roy takes it on mug, reels, catapults back, crack,
thud, bandit slides off wall like slung mud. Then, tooled
boots, bathed, Dale at side, beautiful buttons, croon
Happy Trails, Gabby Hayes…hell, you think I'm not
nostalgic, you think I'm cold transaction with ledger,
balance sheet, hollow drum breast, let me disabuse, I
yearn for television cowboy, Saturday morning marvel
with tin sheriff star, your God feels, too, you think I
like my birth-death machinery, slick wet entrances,
hard dry falls, my inexorable box of flywheels, sprockets
with me at helm punching out screws, I long for cliff-
hanger serial—Captain Marvel, Fu Manchu—absorption
thrill of six year old, then Sunday afternoon Chicago
Bears with buddies, dog, Let me tell you I'm sick of
dazzling brain, omniscient wisdom, Peter's indiscretion,
Stephanie's addiction, give me Davy Crockett, sanitized
binary simplicity. Adoring chesty wives, pioneers. Yes,
nostalgia, not this laborious managerial office beyond
Microscopium and Pyxis in frigid regions. Roy, crisp
embroidery, flash's boyish grin. Let peace rein in great
globed mind free of executions, absolution. Pretty pony,
jangling spurs, hand tooled boots is all I ever wanted.

10.

I want to be like you, mortal, libidinous, breakable. Per-
fection nauseates. I want dismissal for incompetence—
dejection, suicidal. I want to upchuck on New Bedford
Boulevard after mashing a minor. You think I prize
my prodigious bazooka, hydrogen bomb throb? I
want arteriosclerosis, foggy cerebellum. Rescue me
from this. Yesterday I earthquaked Haiti, mud-
slid Peru, arrested pancreatic, faced the billion-needled
human prayer. Give me impotence, grief, deceased
father, rotten teeth. Give me dog requiring euthanasia.
I want eye-bags, uretic sleep. Shell has left jelly; I
am snail on hot concrete, eye dots, brief case, bacon
McGalaxy, mounting office of monotonous colleagues
identical to me. I love them terribly. News descends
like hail: invasion, tornado, prize winner, death.
Alexandra delivers quintuplets. Occurrences assail
people, but I alone in tower must generate each,
welcome or accursed. Get me out this. Only you
with your whorish fake lashes, condom foil, dealer-
ship cackle know how. I am deathless, exhausted.

God eats Diazepam
God weeps spontaneously
God detests blender whine
God withstands unwanted fantasies
God spree killer
God loves middle finger
God wears dog collar
God embodies Germanic neuroses
God worships toilet paper
Gods' father's spermatozoa mashes egg
God adores poultry yolks
God doodles boxes, compulsively—
Coffins, prisons—
God's fat, sick of Milky Way
God wants new zoological facility
God imagines new dominant species named Xyctclut Sapatinne
God imagines no forbidden fruit, episiotomies
God's commitment peters before completing blueprint
God polishes Double Stuff column
God dozes before Bonanza
God despises His decrepitude
Stomps rubies into dust
God wants AC Cobra
Side oilers
Edelbrock
God floods Colorado, delights in property damage
God bowls tsunami over Sumatra, sniggers
God embodies sadistic proclivities
God revels in slaughtered elephants, frozen marriages
God creates child rape like clanging Jeopardy board
To which God ejaculates magma
Hope says God is *tour de force*
Faith hope's handmaiden
And God mists for vulnerability
Let there be and arrives penicillin, interferon, streptomycin
God programs revulsion into lip kiss
Everywhere screams ambulance, fire truck
God, watching triage, pops Corn Nuts
Deposits biohazard in dumpster
Hell with it
I'll devour what I wish
God bellows into cosmos *I AM GOD*

No bull shit
God utilizes cattle car, holocaust
Fluttering missives
God acquires Bugatti Veyron
Black, orange, 1200 HP
Floors it through firmament
God fornicates with Pleiades like bull's seven cows
What's silkier than bovine vulva?
God smokes Metropolises
"Asshole," in chaise under breath God's son mutters
Hearing, God bursts off john, fists bared, charges ingrate
Flying spittle
Polished Florsheims, starched boxers
"Fascist," levels God's progeny, indifferent
Omniscient is God
God never loved, knows it
Lord and Master, King
Monster to wife
Wants to throttle her
Refrains, continues show.

XXXVIII.

Physical existence disappears.
Dense protoplasm thins to bubble
Which, wobbling off wand, widens,
Bursts, disappears.
Biologist theorizes: flesh's futile momentary refusal to accept
Extinction of personality contained within,
While theist, scornful of materialism, understands
Personality ascends to God
Invisible to humans though God perceives
Through night vision goggles
As beautiful streak
Exiting cavity.
God awaits sweet human essence.
Until such mutual gratification heaviness of labor pain,
Mastication, cellular invasion, evacuation,
The incalculable incoherent complexity of continuance.
But walls stretch, burst—
Georgette's lips, Pamela's hips—
In sparkling air.
God's magic trick.
It's imperative, requisite.
Herbert's next, then Junior commanding diesel shovel.
It's bitter medicine: inflation, detachment, translucence, disappearance.
To theist divine.

At university pub God, drunk, mashes high school junior.

Stopped by cop for DUI, God, bladder-urgent, urinates in car.

Later, furious at ex-wife, hurls through windowpane phone

Which dangles over frame like eye and optic nerve.

Next God smashes shoulder through wall.

He despises ex-wife, frigid bitch repulsed by fellatio.

God worships fellatio.

God imbibes at The Globe, the philosopher's bar.

Bleary-eyed pontificates existentialism.

Futility, disobedience, damnation. Gesticulates.

Revelers tolerate God

With his filthy beard.

Institution. Predictable eternal patron

While flocks graduate, vacate,

Make room for new initiates.

Invariable episode: charming smarminess,

Revolted victim, drunken self-expulsion,

Deepening ache of emptiness.

Endearing colorful nuisance.

Flunked compulsory curriculum but devoured unrelated fiction.

God loves the whole shebang:

Diary entry, February 12th: *My failure is loving indiscriminately.*

Nobody understands God, alone at Globe beer-insensate

Who slips melancholic onto street after closing.

Students blow past him like shaken Michelob popped open

For life that awaits them, God hugs.

He mustn't phone her, rip scab.

Futility of spousal reconciliation.

Hopelessness of penetrating stone.

Slip under eyelids. Sleep. Arise. Clothe.

The infuriation of unappreciated genius.

XL.

God officiates game of musical chairs
Across worldwide precincts everywhere.
My parents played with contemporaries, first dozens
of chairs, then fewer, then two chairs with
three players, themselves, Sylvia. When music
stopped Sylvia disappeared. Then my parents circled
one chair, when God lifted needle mother
disappeared. Gleefully, I think, God giggled.
Finally daddy walking round nothing collapsed to floor.
Twenty years later I am walking round numerous chairs:
Alice, Helene, Jim, Susan, Nancy, Tim, Ed, Elaine,
Roberta, Michael, *people try to put us down, talkin'*
bout my generation, why don't you all f f fade away,
we scramble for chair. Blanche! poor Blanche!
Sometimes interminably plays music.
God, I surmise, rubs hands, greedily.
Occasionally God throws child into game,
little plucked chicken who usually loses,
stoically.
Eliminated chairs jam perimeter like exterminated roaches.
Dizzy Gillespie blows jazz, we jitterbug circling,
Orgiastic.
Cartoon cannibals, bone in hair.
Wolves.
God organizes musical chairs among
manageable numbers, countable cadres.
Dinners out, bridge, trophy fishing, cruises, anniversary bashes.
Hymie, Edith, Elaine, Irving, Margie, Sheppard,
Roslyne, Ed.
Once sensual vacationers in Port Aransas.
God's big finger lifts needle off Benny Goodman
and all but one sits guiltily in chair.
Judy succumbs to pancreatic cancer.

XLI.

I make love to God, unnatural for me as I am not
homosexual. I do this as pilgrimage though other
men's erections repel me and God's is especially
clammy, brutal, like wet lead bludgeon protruding
from barbs. I suck it like supplicant, he bloodies
my anus, relishing. I am made female debased by
King for initiation into cult. Henceforth I shall
plead in squeamish architecture oval-mouthed,
cradling hymnal, and bend over naked to his will.

XLII.

God is light, she says.

No, God, he says, is dark, indubitably.

But God, she says, is sunlit interplay on meadow.

God is rock's underside, he insists.

Come again.

What's lies under rock: cold clammy clay.

No, she says. God is ocean sparkle, leaf shiver.

What lies beyond sun, he inquires?

Meaning?

Beyond sun's lumens. What's out there, intergalactic?

Darkness, he answers himself. Black void.

So?

God is that. Microscopic Earth shimmers in solar explosions but darkness—power, greed, ignorance, cruelty—which is God envelopes pinprick of shimmer.

Then you are severe hostile territory.

No, it's you with your belief that grace, love, charity dominate and shall conquer human blight in apocalyptical rainbow-splayed light.

Oh, Bernie, such cynicism.

Oh, Aquarius, such naiveté.

Then can we love each other?

But you are so ephemeral, childlike.

And you an egotist. But I could love you, yes, she says.

But I am tortured, cheerless—dark. Does love trump this?

No, she says, I like your ass.

And I your tits.

And the festering evil rock screams through nothingness.

XLIII.

God says, don't care who you are,
Pablo Picasso, Michelangelo, Billy Shakespeare,
Botti-fucking-celli,
You're repulsive ignorant asses
Clamoring sewer pit of incompetence.
Chest-thumping big shot fashion photographer,
Vogue Elle Mademoiselle with your fancy gadgetry—
Ashes.
God says fuck yourself with your blast-off, NASA craft—
Campfire spark.
And your clumsy angles,
Precious penetrations,
Sacred histories:
Declarations,
Proclamations,
Perseverance,
Heroism—
Pumped up antlion
In conical pit
flicking dirt plume
Of insignificance.
You Van Cliburn, Yo-Yo Ma
Jammed with clayey machinations
To crowing critics
Themselves plumped skeletons.
Locusts burst from preachers' mouths.
God says, don't care what brand of genius,
Big bang theorist,
Stem cell biochemist,
Victorian harpsichordist,
I steam press your chest
To My will,
Stiffening you obedient
Like castigated child,
Restoring me to omnipotence.
Your patents,
Spasms,
Babies,
Velocity,
Catharses,
Victories, and
psychopathological histories

Aren't worth a fish-lip.
Death-gripping your manubrium,
I rip you down
Into dust
Like beaten beast
For the biological kill,
Mercilessly,
your God, Creator, and Destroyer.

XLIX.

I am God, God says angrily.
I am God, another God rebuts.
No, I am God, says God number three.
Undaunted, true God stands, announces primacy.
In rapid succession innumerable Gods pop, Jack-in-Boxes, to
Proclaim authenticity
Bewildering public.
Behind backdrop God laughs sardonically.
But behind this phony splutters God.
Then God says, screw this shit, and murders shrillest charlatan
Starting mass slaughter in which
Gods kill each other unrestrainedly
Unleashing on stage gore-smorgasbord.
Gods pump life from slit aortas.
Audience titters.
One man in orchestra stabs neighbor's eye
Who dies in paroxysmal waves.
Others, brothers in politics, form rival gangs
Each slaughtering each.
Gods on thrones savor holocaust.
Salivate
As if heaping smorgasbord plates.
Glands pre-lubricate.
Now within crammed locked playhouse continuous grisly massacre
With distant aloft deities savoring
And the true Adonai omnisciently everywhere making derisory snapping
Sound with mouth like mocking child.
I am vengeance saith this God
Jealous filicidal sadomasochistic King of Kings
Who summarily, irrevocably turns His back
On the perpetual orgiastic butchery.

L.

He performs miracles.
He resurrects.
He walks in light.
He shows the way.
Some denounce but most join flock.
He inspirits, lives eternally.
His thumb points up or down.
He law giver, supreme judge.
Men pen volumes
But he is uncontainable.
Men slaughter pigs, execrate.
Men decorate eggs.
Shops chock iconography.
He causes disaster flare-ups,
Rubble, mud, debris.
Sun smiles through cloud-lips.
Doxology.
Forms ovals of young mouths.
Inserts under skin like lozenge or lithium battery
Neurocortical transportation.
Surgically gloved he tail-flings into pit
Verminous heretic.
Hollows sequoias into organ pipes.
Many shoot finger, weep in loneliness.
Many jab icy vodka into vein.
Yea though walk,
Squeeze blood over glass blade,
Stab between ribs.
Homogenizes biological father.
Thou art I.
He heals dire.
He refuses hip.
Is pitted hammer-face, missile nosecone, grass blade.
Is Blistex.
God worms into brain, whispers deepest wishes,
Ecstasy, cleanliness, obedience, order.
He possesses magic.
He transforms predictability.
He oxygenates lungs.
Cradles rotting flesh, wins bloody victories.
Makes morning like fried egg.
Noon like fluffy whites,

Evening like a yolk tumbling through gin.
Loves you,
Lifts you,
Places you gently on feathery bed
Or juices you abruptly
And indifferently
in crumple of crashed steel.

LI.

…and this little god cried wee wee wee wee all the way home
which is unusual, for gods seldom scream home afraid
to mommy being immortal, omnipotent, impervious
to pain, imagine Zeus sucking thumb, clinging to mother's
apron under bully-pursuit. Imagine Neptune in water
wings. But chill climbed little god at something unspeakably
evil escaped from pit, red skinless muscle and gut joined
by enzyme-shiny fangs. This little god full of cock girded
for fight but caved bloodless like any coward at implacable
dominance. This thing can strip you off bones like sleeve
of meat discarding pile of steaming guts, so wee wee wee, god's
springy piggy tail corkscrewed up asshole as he flees. Mom,
cookie-warm, wields rolling pin like club, don't fuck with
this, slapping cudgel in hand, nasty piss-ant, crack you
like tick. Piss-ant pops tollhouse, pops mommy's head
between jaws, brains running out like burst egg, slashes
to neck her cunt, sticks head inside, gnashes guts, spits
out ribs. God unshelled nakedly stands—little chubby
package—and is gone in an instant but for chewed
gristle. The other four, like toes: the walls look like
tomato puree blender disaster…

LII.

Jesus perches in Sunday pew. Can't believe this,
He thinks, who is that charlatan up there? And
these parishioners whose minds I read filthily
fantasizing dominance. Listen to Selectman:
fuck shit out a her. Or Pillar of Community:
  I want, thinks Jesus, to wretch.
And what's that crucifix with me peering down
like the Nazi eagle? You believe this shit? And
such mood manipulating garbage: candles,
organ, vestment, apse. I want to rip off roof
to open sky. If God were an ox, that man
in his Breathe of Gethsemane prayer shawl
is God's butcher, and this his abattoir. Hear
his fantasy: *I am God's mouthpiece.* Therefore,
unto you I say, pluck out eyes, cut off tongue,
benumb sex, cauterize mind, stumble dumbly
through world. You are but a thumb-smear
across eternity. These are the only words of
mine ever transcribed which are genuine.

LIII.

To make the poor feel gooey about poverty
Jesus presents heaven. They lose game of
life, win game of death. Hurrah! When asked,
Jebediah of Scytopolis gnawing lizard, sand
frog, whose wife slurps bedsores how jubilant
he is about ultimate ascension, cries, "fuckin' A!"
follows Jesus to Jerozolima, bloody-footed.
Peter is there planning advertising blitz in-
cluding scratch card jackpot. Elisheba, Jeb's
helpmeet, plucking locust wings, hums to
herself, knowingly. Jesus scrapes off street
thronging derelicts, spreads them butter-like
upon his crust: camel, rich, heaven, he intones;
blessed, meek, kingdom. What steam! What
metal! Hunger, righteousness-filled. Sucks
believers out domiciles across grasses to
The Mount, murmuring livestock munching
fava beans. Exalted shall ye be thou des-
perate, dehydrated, persecuted masses. He's
seen, understands the fatuous enslaving
totalitarian bastard—big megalomaniacal jellies
for monotheistic thumbs. It's a wonderful
day. Satisfaction, rapture, God's new heaven.
Savoir reclines in sun-brilliant gratification.

LIV.

God in jammies at ten AM answers
Door on which I rap.
God, I say, heal my crack head son,
Dance him down sober path.
Fuck yourself, he retorts.
God, if you must refuse son,
Restore excitement
To my tedious life.
Bite butt, he exclaims.
I feel like Kirby salesman.
Could you at least, I relent,
Grant me that oceanfront cottage—
You know the one—
Boothbay, Maine.
Buzz off, he grunts,
Slams door.
He did look, I admit,
Indigestive.
I'll come back.
He appeared bilious.
Still, what callous bastard.
Refrigerator Dad.
I'll commit charitable deeds
To gain graces,
Volunteer at Loving Hands,
Buy family a goat,
Infect stranger with joy
Who will infect another
To epidemic in Timbuktu,
Beautifying world.
I'll have that cottage.
I'll see son in Narcotics Anonymous.
Spine shall thrill
With unceasing love.
There are innumerable ways
To charm a King.
Next morning hauling slaughtered ox
Of unblemished character
I call again.
God appears breezily attired, reinvented
As Grand Prix driver.
Here, he says, dashing,

Flips me key.
Attic locker, he says,
Contains total wisdom.
Have at it.
I'm off to Monaco.

Biographer's Postscript.

His son hanged himself at 56.

*Soon thereafter he followed in death
his wife of 64 years.*

He never got that property.

LV.

Oh, I have slipped surly earth bonds, giggle-
silvered wings, done things you've never
dreamed, wheeled, soared, easy grace, un-
trespassed sanctity, reached, touched God's
lash, Oh I have screw-drilled Earth's core,
fantastic threads, done stuff unfathomable,
burrowed, ground, gouged, easy grace,
reached, touched God's anus. Between
BB Earth and heaven stretches God's
torso like Tom Terrific, all else nothingness
where no God rests, shuttle strikes God's
neck, astronaut falls back to Earth, God's
sphincter the isotope pulls all toward, as
if planet were God's legs curled to chin
exposing buttocks. And God protects us
who live within, Carlton, for instance,
whom deadly cyclone overpassed, Madge
whom tidal split round. Countless stories.
Joey whom fire spit to grass, unburnt. Oh,
I have slipped earthly bonds and screw-
plowed to planet's core like William Peary
on kerosene. And Jesus cleanses leper,
sights blind, heals paralytic, stanches gash,
revivifies dead, God's navel being Cathedral
of Blessed Sacrament Church. I am pious,
have witnessed God's handiwork and
were I astronaut or rock-drill pilot would
touch God's every facet, even His muscle
of waste elimination for it too is beautiful.

LVI.

Jesus Christ! My father death-bed yelps, Jesus
Christ! either to admonish or enlist as if King
would ever genuflect or intercede. In 30 AD
he healed people, but He's sick of that,
now suffering accompanies terminality. No
miraculous finger shall touch my father
or she adjacent or hospices of devastated
humanity. Why dost thy, they beseech,
hide? While watching this drama God
pops Junior Mints. Post-op Betty after
thoracotomy moans in agony, morphine,
morphine. God giggles as if Rodney Danger-
field skit. The scene shatters into billion
crystal images of the miserable dangling
in webs of tubes. God's uproarious.
Face, Face. Light never slits this cloud.
God didn't interrupt Hutu hacking, Nazi
gassing. He was pushing Sugar Babies.
But let's be fair: God's not anesthesia
for humankind's perishing. Most dead
people suffered. Jesus Christ! My father
yelps, for help, for mercy; none arrives.
He dies guilty, ashamed, and unimpeded.

LVII.

God shields, exclaims soldier of salvation, flashing Him
like firewall before mortality. Mortality shrivels before God
like ancient penis. Death devours flesh, not soul. Flesh is empty
meal for stomach, deepening, not satiating hunger, like
Cheetos. One soul would bloat Death like fire hose gush
down throat. I own Wyatt Earp Sheriff badge, Elite
Black Visa Card, BJ's Warehouse membership, valid car
inspection sticker but defenseless lies my soul—naked
infantryman. I am without armor against bullet. Faith,
he says, is your shield. God intercedes like Kevlar.
Open eyes, heart, be saved. I shut lids, epoxy heart,
cover self with spite, throw myself from prow into sea
of denunciation, plummet into watery abyss. Death
tears off my flesh. What shark leaves pipefish eat,
plankton devour fiber off bones. I am cloud of
underwater feast. Faith repulses beast from breast.
Have you been saved? "Yes, oh yes!" cry billions.

LVIII.

Jesus healed sick, raised dead, exorcised demons
but I find his greatest miracle is winning football
games. Lions, heretofore winless, thrashed
Bengals. Chiefs, underdog, shocked Broncos.
Spectators gasped. God's son empowered Manning.
Never has he clotheslined so beautifully. Squads
of faith attract Jesus who lovingly lay hands on
helmets. Polished polymer drags light-streak
across TV screen. I read about paralytic,
dropsy, leper, blind but nothing approximates
Blaine Gerrard's immaculately timed last minute
game winning arc to Justin Blackmon converting
fans to fundamentalists. I'm Packer brought to knees.
God blesses Favre. Jesus died for sins of those
who denounce gridiron clash: the stiff-necked
unclean proud miscreant. All one need do is
review football's Hall of Fame: Larry Csonka,
Dick Butkus, Franco Harris, Deacon Jones,
Ray Nitschke, Y. A. Tittle, Earl "Greasy"
Neale. Each one drank the blood of Christ.

LIX.

One proves God's existence by citing the stinking garbage
Dumps of Lagos, Nigeria; Fresh Kills, NY; Bordo Poniente,
Mexico, Great Pacific Garbage Patch, Pacific Ocean.
Mountains of teeming human blight: humankind's
temples riddled with scavengers, bulldozed into mounds
thick as Pyramids. Here lies altar, chancel, transept,
sacristy, Eucharist, scepter, wriggling masses. Pilgrimage
of diesel engines belching black repentant fume like
thunderous guilt, depositing spermy blankets, bloody
towels, expelled placentas, vomiting couches, frizzy wigs.
Priests preside these cresting seas. God forgives. God
absolves. Come unto Me. Dogs shit upon these Pews,
gulls pull coagulated fat. This our ark. This our craft.
Board it now wretched sinners. Here lie rotten ratty
pants, here loafers stiff as husks, here's plastic sucked
by lips. No greater proof than this. Let us, then, gather
round these sewers, shiver humbly, and worship God.

LX.

I ask God directions to heaven. Right at yew tree, he points,
can't miss it. Infernal map fills windshield like atomic
fission. Yew trees ubiquitous. You damn well can miss
it, I smirk. Manically, I tear down dirt roads, dead ends,
psychotic dogs, concrete Jesuses. I pound steering wheel,
shriek obscenities. Fucking goddamn fucking shit!
Hyperventilating, I accept defeat. I lose interest in Paradise.
I'm fried frog under magnifying glass, stinking, sizzling.
Broke. Unemployed. Again I pray, God, make it simple,
I'm lousy at directions. He scrawls picture of nonexistent
road—nothing—New Mexican drought. I slam knuckles
against dash. One bleeds. I'm quotidian, another primitive
beast enslaved by need. I flail like maniac. Heaven is
insurmountable. Signposts, trees, streets, faith; dripping
mayo onto seat I wolf Sonic burger. I just want love,
security, decent bath. I fantasize The Ritz Honeymoon
Suite. I buried invulnerability with both parents. I'm
common bloke, sixty-four, disgruntled. Tattooed people
crawl about like sexualized lizards. I awake each morning
with renewed energy. Point me, God, heart craters.
I'm insistent. Possessed of new vigor, invariably, I end
up screaming. Now steaming radiator halts pursuit.
I stumble into Jamba Juice, sip Island Strawberry, read
Oscar Hijuelo's Mambo Kings Sing Songs of Love. So
many poets like industrial lube squeezed through
cogs, Columbia, Goddard, Warren Wilson College,
Irvine, Amherst, Iowa Writers Workshop, Florida Inter-
national. Futility sweeps across my face. I hate myself.

LXI.

God says, pass, you lived admirably—
loved, forgave, prayed, sacrificed.
Then God says to another, you, back
off! You're condemned. You cheated,
raged, strutted, begrudged. You shall
blister. The consigned one pleads
on deaf cochlea. Trap door bangs.
He plummets to pit of wailing skulls,
boiling flesh, bubbling cauldron
within which sinners eternally
scream. Like fuel, new sinners slide
down shoot. Satan resembles Mr.
Kurtz. Mad, utterly, heads on
pikes. Meanwhile he who passed
gorges divinity, virgins, beefcakes,
girls. Satan bathes in bone
liquefaction. Bartholomew washes
believers' feet. I, Jew, decide to
marry Jesus in formal ritual:
Baptism. Transubstantiation.
Rapture. Reinvention. This I
saw in Ezekiel-like vision: angels
floating round Virgin Mary levitating
above floor of crawling adders.
God said come. I approached.
She bore two faces: one anterior
angelic, beatific, one posterior
grotesque, evil. God commanded
kiss her evil face, kiss Mary's
monstrous ego, kiss her
festering oozing sore. Love her,
he demanded. Suddenly charioteer
lopped off my head, tossed it to
God who jamming digits into
jellies, gullet, with my ropy
member naked, flopping bowled
me over with my own globe into
whose mouth involuntarily I
shat again and again in liquid
terror. Upon awaking I married
God in formal ceremony and
ever after worshipped the
filthy, repulsive, and abominable.

LXII.

Oblong bald tuber above seatback,
I sit in church like Mr. Potato Head ready to play.
Hymn 321 affixes to face my shiny white lips.
Scriptural reading clicks in red nose.
Everybody notices, outrageous.
"Insult!" "Mockery!"
Coherent sermon sticks black derby atop pink pate.
"Blasphemous infiltrator!"
"Who invited him?"
I swivel, smile.
Rouge grins back.
Otherworldly gazes conjoin worshippers.
Love in distillation.
I without antecedent, referent.
What is love? Who is love?
My russet head protrudes like Idaho.
Why here with my conspicuous machinery?
Beauty swells. Everyone fuses into single spirit.
Collectivity against malevolence. Interdiction against frail.
I am mass produced polymer potato with one-piece boots.
Number 31 in Voices of Praise Hymn Book,
"Blessed assurance, Jesus is mine!
O what a foretaste of glory divine!
Heir of salvation, purchas'd by God,
Born of his spirit, Wash'd in his blood"
Punches into me gleaming ears, gloved hands,
Moustache, gaping eyes like shiny hard candy.
I am fully assembled
Planted on pew
In legless un-grace,
Disassociated
From smooth blended mixture—
The poured malted frappe
Of religious compassion.
Lacquered plated alien, I clack to reception
For tollhouse and cider.

LXIII.

God slides muddy mountain face
Burying dozens.
God stomps earth's spine, tsunami
Crushes thousands.
God weeps, drowning village.
God churns cream into hurricane
Displacing half million.
God pounds table mangling one-hundred thousand.
God adjusts thermostat freezing millions.
God shakes blanket capsizing tanker.
God delivers eviction notice, earthquake swallows
Eight-hundred thousand.
God sucks Lucky Strike, seventy-thousand
Of famine die.
God rubs socks on carpet electrocuting
Fifteen hundred.
God burps. Seventy-thousand suffocate in volcanic cloud.
God farts asphyxiating seventeen hundred
With carbonic acid.
God clog dances rocking China.
God bats planetary crib-mobile, sun's force on moon
Stiffens rogue wave.
Man wants piece of land, murders thirty million.
Man purifies tainted blood
Gassing thirteen million.
Man writes children's book, slaughters
three million infidels.
Hutu throws tantrum, vivisects
Eight-hundred thousand.
Man watches Mr. Wizard, blisters
Hiroshima's collective face.
Man burns isotope against
Anticyclone cold, invisible snake slithers
Into citizenry city hatching daisy chain
Of one hundred thousand
Spectacular deformities.
Man victorious atop Mt. Rainier's pinnacle
Guzzles Polar Springs
Creating the Great Pacific Garbage Patch,
Man treasuring ivory box, ivory billiard ball, ivory chopstick
Pumps .600 magnum Nitro Express into
Elephant's kill zone

Twenty-two thousand times a year,
Man adores friendly chat—electroshocks,
Water-boards, freezes, sleep-deprives
Strappado-hinges interlocutor in Uzbekistan's
Jaslyk House of Torture.
God created man.

LXIV.

From pavement God retrieves my soul thugs
kicked out me like eyeball. My soulless body
crumples on curb, face beaten, misshapen.
God cradling soul in kerchief commands,
"steady, faith," and magically reinserts soul
into socket. Life jumps into focus: expressions,
contours, angles, textures. What hit me?" I
ask. "Fear, arrogance, bigotry, hatred, He
responds. Indifferent ignorant killers. But I…
I'm merely…" Understood," God says, "but
you notwithstanding." God fades, disappears.
Noise, grit, heat, glare. I stumble home to
wife with our new Bopper Chopper.

LXV.

I acquire manuscripts for renown publisher.
I reject God's autobiography. Fatuous,
I say, preposterous. No context, no
antagonist. Springs omnipotent from
nowhere. People aren't stupid. This is
unmitigated phantasmagoria. I
recommend mentor, low-residency
MFA, Warren Wilson College, Bennington.
You have spunk but no authenticity. I
could cite innumerable infractions
from confabulism to effrontery.
Witness Chapter 1: grandiosity, brute
contrivance: claptrap. Respect reader-
ship intelligence. Frankly, you write
like pile driver: Chack! Chack!
Chack! Cracked concrete. Unsubtle,
reflecting philosophical immaturity.
We at Octopus Brothers accept
highest quality, limited slots, fiercely
competitive. We wish luck
in placing…I am remorseless.
Script is garbage. Clamoring masses
and their drivel, misguided
drooling Neanderthals. Caricatures.
You and your incredulous procl-
amations, melt back into miasma
of humanity What poisons people,
ordinary unremarkable people,
with grandiosity? I want to weep.
Regarding your mediocrity I say
Embrace anonymity, merge into
the numberless masses, defer to
the masters, apply your unexception-
al Abilities to attainable practices,
be happy in your limited existence.

LXVI.

I confess sins to plastic bathroom scale
I have abused, abominated
Partaken in orgiastic abandon
The dial spins like Satan's head
God is unsympathetic
Real bastard
I have ripped foil wrapper
Popped bubble sack
Wafted clouds of buttered corn
I have blasted Shasta
Of pornographic graft
I lied to gut
God insults dignity
Pay, he commands
I look shamed into his face
Disbelieving
God says you detritus, cloaca
Trash wad
God metes swift implacable retribution
I loathe myself
I want to knife slabs off soul
Large-animal butcher
I am standing upside down
Upon scale of heaven
And am deficient
God hands me machine resembling
Islamic astrolabe
Whose mater calibrates celestial position
Measure, he says
The weight of forgiveness
and the vast star-smear of human love
I point it at sky, ethereal images jump
Into prominent brilliance
And am suddenly absolved of the specific tyranny
Of flesh.

LXVII.

Who created cosmos: God
Who sparked first life: God
Who stuffed baby in womb: God
Who created earth, water, light, dark: God
From whom do flowers bloom: God
Who numbered beasts: God
Who invented human: God
Who gave human dominion: God
Who wins wars: God
Who loses: Satan
Who bestows life-everlasting: God
Who received spikes through wrists: Jesus
Who is omnipotent, omnipresent, omnibenevolent: God
Who quakes earth, slides mud, bowls tsunamis: God
Who selects survivor: God
Who praises God: survivor
Who hoodwinks God: nobody
Who prepackages plague: God
Who thumbs up, down: God
Who devised rigor mortis: God
Who provides abundance: God
Who withholds precipitation: God
Who liberates lager skeleton: God
Who piles skull pyramids: Antichrist
Who spoke after death: God
Who mops man with his corpse: Jesus
What is rapture times infinity: God
Who's bigger than eternity: God
Who masturbates with Vaseline: abomination
Who puts before God calf: infidel
Who holds gun to God's head, execrates: desperado
Who dispatches desperado: God
Who invented child abuse: God
Who incubated another's chattel: God
Who apprehended, executed God: None
Who apprehended, executed sapling: God
Who gave man figs, barley, pomegranates: God
Who condones slaughterhouse: God
Who got hanged by scrotum for diabolism: nobody
Whose sequined cape drapes roof: God's
Who has no face, intestine: God
Who hears God speak: charlatan

Who bore billfold, money clip, shoe horn: Magi
Who invented Christmas: Christian
Who distributes "Jesus"-"Magi"-"Jesus"-Magi" flicker card: proselyte
Who wins Super Bowl, World Series, Masters, Grand Prix: God
Who's plowed under rubble, mud, ash, earth: Pride
Who whores, swindles, robs, lies: the blind
God scorches flesh of whose: man
Who struts in Hugo Boss, Ray-Ban, Officine Panerai: God
Who permeates St. Luke's Episcopal, Presbyterian Intercommunity, Beth Israel
Deaconess, City of Hope caressing, succoring, sentencing, condemning: God
Who devours microwaveable creamed spinach: man
Who honors neither father, mother: God
Who loves, loathes like yin-yang figure: man
Who strives to godhead with monumental, cathartic, orgiastic failures:
Michelangelo, Beethoven Rembrandt, Dostoevsky
Who despoils, fornicates, murders, heals, eliminates, swindles, sacrifices, cadges,
    eats fingernail, dies for cause, deserts, gorges, gouges, loves, destroys, hates,
    repents, creates, execrates, shudders, waltzes, and absolves: Equally and
    simultaneously God and man in schizophrenic, hypomanic, arterially flooding,
    anorectic, physically and spiritually starved obese, spooning, fertilizing, frenzied,
    and afraid in the vine-tangled, gas-stagnant, swamp-mangle of the world.

LXVIII.

God identifies only woman worthy of seed,
Mary rinsing panties in river, unsuspecting
illiterate with ragged nails. Cut her open in
C-section, extracted baby like whole boiled
chicken. Full-blown red clotted neonate
bawling at Mary's tit. Boy Jesus beheading
garters, disemboweling frogs, sling-shattering
light bulbs, devouring AC Comics. Spy Vs.
Spy. Chesty swaggering thing refusing
broccoli. Joseph smacks him. Mary wants
peace from hellion. Oh, the occasional
trip to Swenson's or the hilarious quip
mixes bag. It isn't all horrible. Joe couldn't
afford orthodontics, boy goes gap-tooth,
butt-ended by school toughs, the wire-
mouthed rubber-band ones. Typical. Until
sissy perceived brass and pulling twelve
behind lit into desert. Miracles, sermon,
baptism, crucifixion, martyrdom resurrection.
Throne he sits, immemorial, thirty-three,
barely mature, playing Mortal Kombat,
receiver of prayer uprush. Three-headed
dragon blowtorching world. Yet deep
in root, root within root, love-sap climbs,
love goo, gluing together dichotomous
people, layering, super-fusing—plasma
lamination, inter-oxygenation in contra-
distinctions of destruction and regeneration.

LXIX.

God wraps brilliantly-scaled serpent
round knowledge tree, charismatic,
schooled in brinksmanship; hisses
disarmingly, "knowledge is power,
elucidation mind-blowing, vision
behind veil wrap-around hallucinatory
virtual reality of divinity and fact. You
are magnificent lioness worthy of limit-
less endowment awaiting release.
Uncage yourself. Slay captor. Taste
fruit's succulent meat. And soar
past flesh, fear, inhibition, earth
into delirious space, freedom incarnate,
intoxicant." God's hand wears
sock-puppet Eve, prances her to
tree, exposes her to Mr. Honey Tongue,
widens her jaw, clamps it round
amazing sphere. God, sadistic, craves
subjugation, shame, simpering
repentance of incorrigible sinner.
King of Kings, Almighty Host,
Shepherd, Provider. Comply, walk
humbly, prostrate deprecatingly,
gaze up adoringly from God's silky
lap pillow, tip-curled tongue panting
at His unknowable icy twinkling.

LXX.

I was faring swimmingly—woman hair-washed
feet, infirm glowed, deceased rose, food-fish
teemed in nets, throngs converted—without
you. You couldn't leave it alone, stuffing me
with pudding, over-gloating, pumping with gift-
bearers. I was satisfied, functioning. I didn't
need your head stuck in my details. Predictably
you snuffed my happiness, bribed friend to
rat me out, mortified flesh, nailed me shut
under mocking sign: "King of Jews." (Why
through wrists and not, sadistically, balls
or tits; you always resented me.) Such splendid
revenge, subsuming me eternally under your
fluff, suffocating me. Granted my swollen
egotism, but needed you lance my lava
out? Couldn't you allow actualization? I was
superb physician, I abated suffering. Selfless,
always selfless, liberator against autocracies.
And you, hateful to the last, stripped my
thunder to bloody bone, stuck me in crib
somewhere near Microscopium. Baby, even
now, into whom you ply universal infantilism.

LXXI.

Men, grease painted, kill each other.
Head, necks thick black streaks. Gangs
Clasping signed, countersigned contracts.
Lone assassins crisscrossing streets.
Rage-fuelled hatred, cartridge, barrel,
Throat-slitting shiv. Rapists, too,
Neck-dragging women by belt behind
Dumpster for spasm. Snow, horse,
Four Roses. Gaudy iridescent tattoos.
One shatters whiskey bottle, twists
In girl's cheek. One crooks fingers,
Rips open victim's mouth. Churches
Groan with prayer. Belfry traps flapping
Hymns. Futility of humble. Innocent
Billfolds split like figs to gun-thugs.
Poet's final vision: moron's pistol
Muzzle. Nothingness. Psychopathic
God lays out with porn, Astroglide,
Levitating over ant bed creation.
Teeming thoraxes, mandibles, legs,
Dragging line of microscopic dung.
Starry God, internet smut, spasm.
Humanitarians mail charity flyers:
Starving children, harelip defect,
Diseases. Goats for family. Donkeys
for drudge. Nobody gives. Death.
God swallows petitions like sludge.

LXXII.

I search for love,

My first stop God:
Charred human skull.

I spread vulva:
Wail echoes walls.

I seek Rinpoche:
Chinese finger trap.

I scratch hole in soil:
Tumescent Caucasian penis.

I surf blue Tahiti:
Rockslide crushes chest.

Biological mother:
Skeletonizing piranha.

Biological father:
Cascading napalm spittle.

Roman Catholic Church:
Olympic mucilage pool.

Intricately carved crucifix:
swinging bull scrotum.

Slit my jugular:
Rust.

Surely, chocolate raspberry torte:
Mice uproariously giggling.

Recline on TempurPedic:
Clamping crustacean claw.

I pilgrimage to Borobudur, Teotihuacan, Ur:
Empty python eggs.

El Sanctuario de Chimayo:
Box of turkey waddles.

Dirty, broke, fat, I quit in Plainfield, Massachusetts:
Fisher cat unleashes clean horrifying scream.

LXXIII.

1.

Dear Constance,

Thank you for hosting such a wonderful party. The food was marvelous, especially those prosciutto wrapped baked scallops. And where did you find such delectable sturgeon? And, of course, seeing you after so many. Your home sumptuous understated magnificence. I love the library. Is that truly an original Durer? Thank you, too, for including Benjy. I thought he comported admirably given his challenges. I know he felt significant. He so struggles for normalcy. I love, dear Constance, your unconditional humanitarianism. Who was that God-like hunk from Croton-on-Hudson. Relative? Or, no, could it be! Connie, I'm so fatigued. I sometimes wish it were ended. Again daffodils, again hydrangeas, yet no expansiveness. Antidepressants seem laughable. Now insomnia. I reminisce our Barnard days, such idealism. Now Frank's gone, and Charles, misguided Charles. Wouldn't shock me to hear…. I've enjoyed a peaceful morning: Benedictine eggs, cantaloupe. I must start exercising. Do you remember Darlene from Holyoke? Tumbled off a ladder, shattered everything—we're all balsa. At Sunny Horizons Rehab, poor darling. Connie, let's take a Carnival cruise, the Yangtze—Beijing, Xian, The Gorges—you and I. How marvelous that would be. Connie. Don't you see? It's such a shock, reality. Where *is* Holyoke? Think of all that treacherous ice. Sometimes I feel like Bacon's howling Pope. Wouldn't there be weeping cherries? Thank you again for a lovely, you create such approachable elegance. Truly, you are a trusted dear valued friend.

2.

Dear Marjorie,

I think I'm going insane. I feel abstracted, disconnected—numb.
I'm indifferent to demise of others. Monstrous. Sometimes,
when slicing potatoes I fantasize homicide. Intellectualism,
all that obtuse yammering, sickens, such strutting egotism.
Contempt, Maj, is my undoing. History mauls us insensate.
Alien. I love that word, alien, alienation, dispossession. In
one being can existence and nonexistence simultaneously
exist ? Rhinoceroses come to mind. Hippopotami. Immense
lumbering anachronisms. How their joints must ache. Don't
you think everybody knows? Everybody, that is, of maturity?
The pieces one's labor rips out, those brutal offices.
Marjorie, I look at Richard and suffer. His shaggy scrotum
hanging like suicide. Something like melted wax pulls off
in hands. Dick, oh Dick, who is the crucifixion. Don't you
think, Maj, we're all The Christ? Let's lunch tomorrow—
at Leonardo's—please say yes. Since Janie and Donnie evaporated…
I love the risotto. One becomes automatous. Confession:
I have begun to drink. I've told nobody. After Dick leaves.
I do in nightgown with jigsaws—Seurat, Renoir—splash of
Stolichnaya. Naughty me, without velocity. You seem so
knuckled into life, like tires knobbing mud. Envy, perhaps,
after all, I'm not chloroformed, just anger inwardly driven,
self-castigated. Anyway, alcohol pieces me together. Use-
lessness blurs edges. It's me as much as him: Dick and I
never fuck. Do you and Bert? We're bored. One walks
a long way to boredom, past children, passion, purpose,
suffering, past brilliance to the blank cliff face. What lies
beyond boredom, Marjorie? I see exhausted gorgeous
women side-by-side, bereft, barefoot, cold, diving off
earth—sexy pointed toes—into the abyss. Perhaps, after all,
I'm lesbian. Such beautiful fragile souls soundlessly falling.

3.

Dear Caroline,

Since Robbie died I've been summoning God, un-
successfully; when does God ever appear? Lately
I've noticed my big toenail thickening like rhino
horn. Fuck God. I need succor, get frippery.
Christianity sucks. There's no supernaturalism.
Biochemistry is God: depression, ecstasy, despair,
love. I could die of this. Robert and his casting
reels. The man worshipped fishing. Only moments
between thighs bested angling, and of that I'm
insecure. He never warbled there. Vagina now
is strung with spider webs. Brain, too. What an
instrument, the body: organs, skeleton, muscle,
blood dammed by skin. Air sucked through follicles.
Alveoli. What a word: alveoli. Erectility. Copulation,
multiplication. If God were solid like crystal. I
have decanters, platters, candlesticks. What does
one do, Carly? You'd think He'd be available,
like gelato. I'm painting nails today—oxblood,
poppy, Bordeaux lust. I'm thinking of The Rub-
ber Monkey or Wetlands tonight. Interested?
Will Marco let you out? Two cars just in case.
Hell, since Robert it's never been good. He had
such thick fingers. It's back to that: body. Think
of that magic trick in which illusionist passes
hoop round levitating woman—who is me—
disconnected, floating, comatose, proving The
Miraculous. Then curtain falls, rises, magician,
assistant bow on stage to wild applause. Physics
is irrefutable reality. Damn God his little magic
show. At midnight janitor throws final switch
and gravity smashes heavenly bodies to bits.

4.

Dear Penny,

God spoke to me today: I satisfactorily evacuated bowels,
read Death of Ivan Ilych. Not everyone can thusly boast.
So much malnutrition, illiteracy. That I comprehend Tolstoy
in gastrointestinal unawareness is blessing. I am gryoscopically
blueprinted, lucid. When Tolstoy writes, "…Praskovya
Fedorovna was not always conducive to the pleasures
and amenities of life, but on the contrary often infringed
on both comfort and propriety and he must therefore
entrench himself against such infringement," God
blesses me with comprehension. Surely, I am within rights.
I may impute from my advantages God's existence.
My heart pumps perfect pressure, brain withstands
termites. Grace. Vibration. Ecstasy. Pen, I tell thee
I am light; pure helium. One is unaware of one's
beautiful spinning. Penny, Penny, clean summer sun
washes grass. Let's invade the lake, two old biddies spilling
over pants. Who cares about cellulite. We are justifiable
animals. I have two tins of smoked clams. Today God
opened dungeon door and out walked I into blinding
bright. I perceived lips upon my lips. See, I am voided,
right as newborn babe. Honor this child, this widowed
ancient child whom God hath anointed this day April
twenty-seventh, two-thousand fourteen, Anno Domini.

5.

Vapors scud overhead, flimsy as rent rags.

Leafy spears stab, twist into blue flesh.

Nipping wind lacerates naked shingles.

Seven slitherers mass in multicolored pulp.

Dear Lottie,

Please tell me what to do, I'm so alone, shipwrecked
and no God stands before me. This is what it's like,
hopelessness, eaten face at center of nothing, hot
howling. Lottie, you have Bernard and little Bobbie
and I imagine spontaneous hilarity at serving spoon.
Home with jungle gym, hydrangeas while I live in
unit 7-C with Benjamina. I'm too retiring. Too
shamed. I still have mama. I've never divulged: I
paint lips thick, troll for sex. It's dangerous, therefore,
exhilarating. I could be killed. I love strange men
fucking me. It's death wish I surmise. Last Friday I
took two successively. I craved a third. Godless,
abandoned, shut out. I confess to whoredom.
Lottie, I can't. Come tonight. I can't. It's too
horrible. Moldy pages. Lamentation. Psalm. All
mold. You know your Sandy, fragile, shaky. I've
started smoking cigarettes. Am I disgusting?
(My nose is narrow-grotesque.) You are nonjudg-
mental. I have blustery thighs. A little honesty: I
hate myself. Where is Mr. Omnibenevolent One?
You haven't got Him all. Great Cardiologist
to hammer my heart? Open yourself, they say,
He will build nest of love. I have been gaping
for decades to absence of nightingale. Lottie—
Loretta—tell me what to do. You are so in ecstasy.

Earth lashes its back, weeps rivers.

Little green flame-tips cut through death.

Pillow experiences quakes of delirium.

Scream-threaded needle pierces eardrum.

6.

Dear Eleanor,

Progress! God entered me like flashlight squiggle.
I conceived! I carry zygote. Spittle fuses me to
pillow. Savoir Faire, God debonair, God hot
caramel. Me in ecstasy! I am bigger by the
minute. I wear night like stole of diamonds.
Remember my atheism? All slime, onion.
How I coupled with garbage, chin full of gin.
Debauchery, whoredom, Sodom, depravity.
I guffawed like slattern. Now divinity. Tuned
instrument. Sphere within sphere. Gyroscope
whirring. Hail Mary, full of God's semen.
I am sacred. Uncorrupted. Risen. I am loaf.
Into me shoots music, out me lyrics. I love
my rapist's execration who deserves
rehabilitative caressing. Jesus is my aorta.
Redemptive is my murderer. Eleanor, you
see? Life is not mud in doomed nostrils, nor
helium-filled knees of satisfied delusion.
Come to me. Drink my tincture. Open your
stuffed swampy stumps to the Mad Creator.

7.

Dear God

I am sorry I pray like a child—
Now I lay me down to sleep,
I hear no voice, I feel no touch,
Help us do the things we should—
Such canned simple-mindedness—
Yet possess no instruction for wisdom-prayer
Commensurate with physical maturity.
Perhaps You want us stunted,
Wrapped in pre-pubescence gauze
For Your despotic studio.
Heavenly Father, I might plead,
Forbid mastectomy,
Shrink prostate,
Protect Meg.
I might beseech, Dear Apocalyptic One,
Strike Viv's mass benign,
Alone at home with memories.
Arm her antibodies with howitzers.
Is this admirable petition
Or egotistical compartmentalization?
Feed hungry, heal sick, bestow peace
Seems delusional as if mop could
Wash every streak.
Then for my soul alone?
Forgiveness. Absolution. Purification.
Appreciation of my tortured mate.
Dear Father, I am tabula rasa
For Your pastel stick,
Scrawl me
Furious wisdom,
Smear purple prayer
Across my breast,
Gouge with thick profundity
My vascular walls
Into Your abstract masterpiece.

8.

Dear Stephanie and Charles,

I look at you, see God. Devotion so thick,
you would die for each other. You are brick.
Blessing and achievement. Most people,
even coupled, suffer godless loneliness
in atheistic desertification. You walk in
grace sun-gilded. I can only imagine. I
can fantasize. What confidence must be
yours. Staff, sandaled feet is all required.
You are Lamb. While I, dear I…Am
full of soda. How do you do it? Is it
Princeton or inheritance, concerted
psychology? I see you through sixth
iniquity, through venous lens of sin.
I cannot enjoy though your love
envelopes. Oh Steph, Chuck pity
your wretched friend full of Pepsi Zero.
I want to walk in glow beribboned.
Disingenuous to entreat God I reject.
Or might I hedge?—Pascal's wager.
Light and dark play upon your face,
innocence in the precinct of lust,
children. Oh babes, give me pluses.
Honor covers envy like paper rock.
I am transit. Torque flattens my
face. This song is yours my beautiful
best bosoms, leave me to my jigsaws.
(I've almost finished Klimt!) Surely,
aproned God in studio chips away.
I have known men with licorice hair.
My angel blood coats jealousy's jaws.
I have always envied those God loves.

9.

Dear Francine,

Through splattered windshield of atheistic materialism
I've admired people I considered flawless—charitable,
selfless, spiritual, optimistic. I've grown to hate them.
At night God's absence corrodes this infidel. Doubtful
faithlessness's causality, but interesting how this atheist
failed at love. One eats one's self and starves. Franny,
sixty-five years normalizes deficiency. Nobody notices
the ubiquitously visible. I'm still unabashedly, regardless
universe's incomprehensible complexity, godless. I
just am. I grate my spiritual insufficiency into slivers,
willing to disintegrate, but cells crave otherwise. I'm
thick hard core, almost steel. Mystifying that I channel
you from freshman year, nineteen-sixty nine, freckled,
raven-haired coed, surname snapped off mind like
twig. You're cloudy imagery, Jewish sensuality at
dormitory pool. I have gone through many. Franny,
I wonder how life has carried you, cancer perhaps,
emotional trauma? Some muddle unaccompanied.
So long ago we spilled onto Congress, outraged,
chanting antiwar slogans, oblivious to God. Stephanie,
Nancy, Cookie, Todd. I haven't a clue. It matters,
though. History's thick gauze swallows life that
dazzled. I'm too intelligent to believe in God.

10.

Dear Carleton,

We're two mountaineers in motion picture, chests pressed
to rock, forearms locked together over sharp edge of cliff.
I'm rescuing you from tumbling left into abyss, or frame
Tilted ninety degrees you're rescuing me from scraping
down face on right. Foreheads pop beads. Pain yanks
grunt. "Hang tight, got you," we sputter." God's amused
at pitiful climbers desperately co-dependent. We slip
down sweaty muscular flesh. Sturdy fingers, grit. Carleton
saving Gordon, Gordon Carleton. Eternally. God chuckles
at nature's imperative. Brother hauling brother. Grip
broken one would plummet. Tendons rip. "Hang tight!"
The peace we might know, releasing. No grip is flawless.
God smacking Milk Duds bores, walks out—only one watch-
ing—leaving two quivering buggers in unobserved horror.

LXXIV.

Obstetrician God delivers babies into mortality.
God wears green germicidal mask.
God with forceps, vacuum extractor.
Stirrups pry mother's thighs.
God says pant, focal point.
Push, God commands.
God says boy, mortal.
God says girl, mortal.
God says preemie, dying.
God says anencephaly, condemned.
God loves morbidity,
Delivers every baby.
Mommy mortal strolls future mummy.
Black sprigs tuft God's fingers
Gleaming with alcohol scrub
Smashed under surgical gloves
While performing physician ritual.
Placenta-streaked baby
Slips directly into pot
Like skinless chicken.
God smiles.
No spice required.
Birthing cell replicates cozy bedroom:
Brass lamp, bedside table, oak bureau,
Reproductions.
Most mothers suffer hours
In thirst, primal labor,
Inconsolable, desperate, furious
Delivering doomed neonate
Into rapid soma between nothingness
And nothingness—
Davy, Ahmed, Emiko, Abimbola—
Which gratifies God
And accrues to Him
Magical formidability,
Rigid formality.
God bungler
Who craves stillbirth
Must countenance, grudgingly,
Life's momentary triumph
Twisting through birth canal
Like wild isotope.

Damnable affront! God stamps.
Outrage!
Fluttering, screeching
Like cabin-trapped owl
Slamming into walls.
An indignation.
You and your pep, zing, pow.
You and your multiplication.
You and your magnetism.
You think I'm threatened?
I have instruments.
I have inevitability.
I have tragedy.
And you in birth room wrathfully packaging.
I am God.
I am Mortician.
I am Executioner.
I am Master in glittering robe.
Into blue palms babies arrive with blurry eyes. hazy

LXXV.

God shut window between two lovers
Who streak it with blood on either side

God shoulder pad of footballer who
Dislocates cuff running split right scat right 639 F angle

God corporation's executed agreement
Condemning farmland to fallow

God orangeade in amniotic sac
Irradiating zygote with deformity

At amphibious landing from bunker God
Chops down invading children

God, grimacing champion, protrudes neck
Across finish line into garland of human bones

God stethoscope the instant nurse
lifts it off fresh cadaver

Discotheque bomber splatters
On ceiling God's visage

I am atheist proclaims phenomenologist.
I am atheist brags archaeologist
I am atheist propounds primatologist

God first rampant pancreatic cell
Breaking out prison

God's toenail gashes prow drowning dozens

Irma Grese rolls naked with naked Nazi doctor in
Slop of amputated Jewish breasts in gory Auschwitz
Orgiastic bliss while Mengele chemically burns,
Eyeball injects, sterilizes, freezes, vivisects

Inspired by God.

LXXVI

1.

God is cessation of feeling
God is numbness
God is cryopreservation
God is disingenuous prayer
God is blank of neutrality
God does not jive, bop, pancake, flip
God is clothespin
God is paperclip
God is dead battery
God is inspirational diet book
And weight loss plan
Two asphyxiated captains in cockpit
Of passenger jet
On automatic pilot
Flying nowhere—
God is roar, contrail
God is sprinkler water hanging in air before tumbling to chlorophyll
God is guilt tree barren of pears
God is lizard eye tracking fly
God is gaping black sock hat
God is spider web twisted by broom
God is supremacist blue injected into verminous brown
God is blank dictionary
Rage geysers in God's withdrawal
As does love
I have no God, am therefore
I have no God, am forthwith
I have no God, am kinesis
Adonai Elohei-Tzva'ot! Who is as mighty as you, Yah? Your moronity
surrounds you
I am pernicious
I am insidious
I am lugubrious
Hymns fork like serpent tongue
I strike, poison heart with God
M-dash connects clauses of nothingness
I despise my father, denounce The Father
Killing God I killed him
I am fine, gracias
I love word bittern
I love word citron

I love word absinthe
I love Kobo Abe's seductive sand scorpion
I love polished solid agate egg
I cup penis, scrotum in sleep
Do not believe otherwise
Do not imagine otherwise
Do not believe color coded world map wall-tacked
Or silver crucifix dangling
I am lidless eyeball atop shoulders
I am vigilant head-size eyeball
I am God saith Lord
Here, take golden broth
Here, take fatty broth
I have slaughtered ox
I have drained veins
I have sautéed
Here, have wooden bowl
I am your
I am our
I am their
You I love like staple gun
Like effective scissors
Like pottery mug
Above all others
Without God I tremble like he in love
Do not think me Caesar of exhilarated death-thumb
Nor Caligula's orgiastic barbarism
Atheists write greatest exposition
I am whale and whale's antidote, superego and id
I am triple-pronged plug conducing novelettes
I write execrable, internal organs
I write starvation
I read Confessions of Mask, weep
I read Sailor Who Fell From Grace With Sea
I read Marat Sade
I am genius at imitation
God is originality's execution by rope
Friar pulls bell
Bell clangs terminus
Fires ensue
God coldly watches human flesh crackle

2.

Suddenly I am Jesus's disciple
Suddenly I kiss scripture
Suddenly immersed in plentitude
Suddenly fiery sword cuts Gordian knot
Halves split like Fuji
Suddenly immortality's fragile fructose
You who see me
You who smear me
You who extirpate me
Hold my push and pump of modesty
Suddenly I am girl, proud, amazed at swelling breasts
I am preparing for conception
I am soft, widening
Christ's chaste bride in embroidered milk
Suddenly I am clean pencil writing ecstasy
Suddenly I am liar, monster, addict, fraud, user, deceiver, fat boy void of beautiful
    scruple, suffocation lover, body dysmorphic sufferer, blunt cudgel wielder,
    callous bastard wrecking fragilities, rage-filled blaster, razor gilled flicker,
    suddenly I realize I am inhuman like murderous obedient slanderer
Suddenly I realize I am evil
Peas porridge hot, peas porridge cold, peas porridge in pot nine days
I give you peppermint candy ice cream
I give you pop-up book
I give you muffled wrist-pulse
I give you dilation
I give you liquid scripture's pool of magic minnows
I give you yellow pulp like tapioca
I give you Goddess Calliope
Wonderful news
Dopamine rush
Napalm of flowers
Quaver in transubstantiation
Inexpressible succor
I give you nude clothing
Tell me, then
Cleave me, then
Ladle brimful molten soup
For I am rich with cavity
The Christian crack
My broad-groined Centaur

Suddenly I am domestic constellation
The Twelve Starred Timidity
Long lashed, innocent
Select me
Adopt me
Poke me in heart-soil
Way down upon the Sewanee River, far, far that's
I am
Show me
Let's have
God in toes, God in glands, God in fleshly lubrication, God in peristalsis
    elimination, God in mastication, God in hydrochloric acid, God in fat, God in
    cuticles, God in hair, God in corporeal gratification, God in bone marrow, God
    in timbre, God in fibroblast fascia muscle, God in urine, God in brain, God in
    mammalian milk aqueduct, God in knee, God in rump, God in endocrine
    nervous immune, God in hunger consummation and grist
God in man's phantasmagoric godliness
Give suck
Give lamb
Give wine
Give fist
Suddenly I am destitute, luminous, amok

3.

I read Mother Courage and Her Children
I read Biedermann and the Firebugs
I read The Mad Woman of Challiot
I read The Iceman Cometh
I read Henry IV, Blood Wedding, Caligula, No Exit
I read Playboy of Western World
God is mechanical photographic eye
God is rigid magnetic generator
God is spinning reel paying line
God is computer neurotransmitter
God is raw-potato data pushed through straw
God is necessary general anesthetic
I read Macbeth, Threepenny Opera
I have no idea
I have no referent
I whirl in amniotic bath
Abandoned, raw
With Archbishop of Rome
Grand Imam of Mecca
Each of whom knows nothing
But hypocrisy, theater, glove
Ice-prayer
Frozen slush
Cryonic brain plate
Something's there
Sacred ether
Sacred absence
Sacred emptiness
Sacred austerity
Sacred alcohol-clear spreading sterility
Something inspiring, immortal, wordless, terrifying
Deep ubiquitous stalking
Squawk God, squawk God
Iridescent wing beating
In pre-progenitive air
End and beginning
End, beginning
End of tingling transformational feeling
Beginning of rapturous amputated petrification
So it curls, so it curls
In ghostly shapes
And ghostly swirls
Through lungs of the stricken.

LXXVII.

God attending life's last gasp, death's first clasp—
spouse, children, in-laws rush into doom room.
Probate, divvy, claim, haul to dump. Theirs now
dilapidated house, heirloom silver. Painful con-
fessions, pillow tears, naked, exposed. Thorny
matriarch slides off plank into sloshy history.
Survivors bandage fear in pathological gauze—
He will comfort, He soften? Fleshless skulls create
religion, solid iron impenetrable shield. Where
life's force meets entropy's law, at age, say eighty-
nine, the exchange occurs, when brain stops
thinking. "Gone to God," we say, "In God's
bower," if God be ubiquitous hero—and He is.

LXXVIII.

I blow fire into Thor's Pine, Cedar of Montezuma;
Annapurna, McKinley, Chang-Tzu; Black Eye,
Magellanic, Andromeda; Amazon, Nile, Colorado.
What make you, little twits, with your bone-
coffined hypothalamus? Tentacular cancers—
Calcutta , Mexico City, Manhattan, smog-suffocated,
crime-infested, pestilential; luxury liners; transport
trucks oozing axle grease; babies slated for slavery,
exhaustion, failure, extinction; hydraulic shovel
gouging dirt. What arrogance to believe I created
you in My image. What giggle. You striving for
godhead with your Chrysler Building. Such grandiosity!
I could stomp planet like toad pulping your over-
exaggerated pompous croak. Freak, abortion—
unfinished, misshapen, physically paltry. Swamp
of disease. Not wishing you extinct I scatter grain
like barnyard feed amused by your scarlet waddle.
You worship me, I absorb your gushing Sunday
entreat like dirty mop wrung in sink. You deliver
beautiful baby and imagine you're blessed refusing
to perceive the gynecological-obstetrical species
reproducing hatchery. I see your guilty flesh-
centered sins transformed into blood-curdling
disingenuous spiritual hymns. Honesty moves me.
Were you honorable I would waft you to Paradise
on cheek's pink stream, rejoice, finally rest, relieved.

LXXIX.

So used to admiring yourselves in glass, God says,
you imagine yourselves beautiful. Limitations lie,
vanity blinds, delusion requires simplemindedness.
Four waving appendages, blunt forehead, rump,
orifice, nose under eyes, gullet under nose, cartilage
stereophonically jutting forward, gelatin, hair. The
lubricious internal-external reproductive machine.
Beautiful, you exclaim, gazing upon murderous
gluttonous blithering graceless lump of morbidity
and horrific disease—Ebola, meningoencephalitis,
Kaposi's Sarcoma, typhoid, HIV, Glanders, endless
possibilities. I concede you tinker advantageously:
silicone implant, self-starvation, liposuction, and
pew after pew, hands on lap, gazing upward
express prayerful gratitude for advantages. I laugh,
cry simultaneously. From out soup leggy fish with
skull wide enough to admire itself, put on airs,
invent TV and fabulous mythologies. I love you
for engaging, for attributing to me omnipresent
attention and shall never forsake you, my favorite
fragile fabricators for whom I suffer, and pity.

LXXX.

You might be shocked to learn my timbre is bled veal.
Similarly, it will stun you to know I am physically frail—
girlish shoulders, gossamer wrists. If you want veracity,
my penis is eternally soft slug. Finally, remorsefully,
I must inform that I dwell not in you as love or shield,
but rather white shirt, knit tie in fluorescently bathed
office cubicle, expendable company functionary;
there I exist under flickering tube, plodding, defeated.
It might surprise you to know Lazarus's flesh, four
days putrid, stuck to my fingers like gum. Men,
feeding your predatory predisposition , providing
an easy victim of derision, I confess, pathetically,
I have never mounted woman. Shove me down
stairs. Mud awaits my face. It may depress you to
know I affect outcome of no war. Neither succor
suffocating miner nor suffering tumorous child.
Ramadhan stampeders trample me, squash me
in Basilica alleyway. Patriotic graveside supplications
find no benevolent adjudicator. Seek me, if you
must, at Finkelstein, Ogletree, & Botts, LLC, thirty-
third floor, twenty-eighth desk, row one-hundred
four. Think ergonomic chair, pretzel snack barrel.
Despise chasm between fact and fabulist, cosmos-
Father versus beet salad me with touch of Phlebitis.
It may devastate you to see Savior's fungal toenail
or torn anus lip leaking blood on White Cloud.
Go home, expand, cry the poison out your eyes.

LXXXI.

God morphs into locomotive, slams through cloud-me
dragging vapor sheet off engine. God pivots, now
bull, gores me: I splash, recollect tauntingly. God
wants me exterminated, becomes Peterbilt, plows
into me: indomitable singing Rorschach on grille.
What then shall I pray? Father, I am sin, embrace
basest nature—sodomite, partaker. I am obscene.
God becomes elephant, stomps me into ground: I
billow like parachute round toes. God transforms:
battle cruiser, trident rocket, fighter jet—my iniquities
swirl round his cone like spun sugar. Sanctuary
heebie-jeebies. I grin big teeth. I'm God's miscreant
solid as sneeze. God redoubles effort, becomes beastly
heat, one-hundred fifteen degrees. I evaporate in
waves, reconstitute, rain atheism onto cracked
riverbed: victory. God is not without weapons but
refuses further engagement as time wasted on
nasty fucker, clammy from cold bayou mud, bloodless,
freeing me to click down pavements of depravity.
I impregnate girl, adulterate with history professor,
worship craven images, entertain high-stakes
covetousness. God, recognizing goodness under
my lashes and refusing "abandonment of cause"
deploys Ambassador-Son who exercises antidote:
universal love, most fervently bestowed on adversaries,
denunciators, agent-provocateurs, jam on burnt
toast. I have none of it being irrevocably unmiti-
gated. Apoplectic, fascist God visits on me private
holocaust culminating in emaciating self-hatred.

LXXXII.

1.

Please God destroy compulsions: OCD sufferer
I am exemplary, God zap tumor: patient
Moisture, just God: farmer
Club, any club: gambler
Redeem him, God, strike him clean: junkie's s father
Seize this arm, Lord, this perfect arc: quarterback
Gather her, bestow peace at last: gasping mother's son
I'll do anything, God, give me the call: job applicant
Higher power: alcoholic
Shitface! Bastard! Asshole!: new premature widow
Shield, Jesus, enclose my house: wildfire evacuee
Hone me knife edge sleek, unhittable: occupying soldier
Now I lay me to sleep: child
Draw up easy, Lord, gently set down: fearful flyer
Into, my wonderful beautiful Shepherd, the cup: putter
Inspire to favor, Gracious Savior, my proposal: businessman
A: student
Zilch: goalie
Crampon: climber
Steady: surgeon
Daylight: miner
Mama: famine child
Rescue: hostage
Worth: depressive
Identity: refugee
Bull: day trader
In God's hands: power plant operator
Zip-A-Dee-Doo-Dah
Zip-A-Dee …
My Oh…
Wonderful…
Satisfactual
Now is the time, I say, now goddam time
For all good men, I say, for all good men
I feel pretty, Oh, so pretty,
I feel pretty and witty and bright
God says, yes, you
God says, anytime
God says, yesterday today tomorrow
God says, Buster Brown
God says, Betty Boop

God says, meet me in Poughkeepsie

God says blue strawberry Freezie teeth

God says, you and what army?

God says, sloppy drunken slut walking vagina like Pekinese

God says, pseudo feminist intellectual bastard fucking everything that moves

God says, scum bucket, razor blade, poseur, naïf

God says, gamin-heart, bread-flesh, fear-brain

God says, sour apples taste sweeter than human love

God says, not always, not absolutely

God says, duplicitous, double-blooded

God says, of course, exceptions

God says, frailty is name—diphtheria, lymphoma, diabetes, stroke

God says, axis 1 psychiatric disorder

God says, I plump blanket, snuggle

God says, try this pillow

God says, Hav-A-Tampa

God says, drink another tattoo in heartland of terror, do bony maronie

God says, curved fluorescent neon tube

God says, Eat-A-Pita

God says, I am odor fresh deodorizing urinal cake

God says, piss splinters like lemonade

God says, carnality ego-atrophies love—hard artery love, lead pipe love

God says, whomsoever My light touches shall drip liquid fingertip rubies

God says, gullibility guppies whip head into mud

God says, why doth thou hide thy faith?

God says, perception is rigor mortis, speech gas escaping, excretion decomposed
   image, possessed objects coffin handles; faceless pulp-less baggage-less etherized
   nothingness in grocery aisle

God says, mummy tape wrapping infinity

Where, God says, I am

God says, Sewanee River way down upon

God says, *get motor runnin'*
      head down highway
      take world in love embrace
      climb so high
      never wanna die

God says, you dead man

God says, Mattie told Hattie

God says, emblazoned across forehead eleventh commandment: Thou shalt disobey

God says, coconut cream pie

God says, lie on back, arms outstretched, legs ankle-crossed, bleed, cry, flesh rip, sag
   like rag, barbed wire hat, tongue loll, rot

God says, holocaust is raw truth, grinding mill stones, human seed sown across
world, grass blades, hay

God says, last one there's rotten egg

God says, snuggle down, fetal position, curl under my eider sweet baby, dream
ice cream mound, caramel butter cup, that is all there is dearest innocents,
nothing more, this, yet not even this, you are not just already decomposed flesh
or a metaphor for decomposed flesh but the illusion of the illusion of death and
decomposed flesh, oh my tragic darlings

Rub-dub-dub

Three men in tub

Ran up clock

Ran down clock

Three blind mice

Oh please God, oh please forgiving generous-hearted God, I shall ask for nothing
ever else, just grant this, this one loving-kindness gift at this moment on this
lonely revolving orb in this singular broken bed in Plainfield Township among
red maple, white ash, oh just this from such a potent hand easily accomplished
beneficent act

Timidly, like mouse

Nose twitching

I love nature's colors, I mutter

Yellow, pink, white, blue, black dapple scattered onto spectrum cresting green
washing eye in blurry smear of tumbling brilliance, timidly, I say

I inhale prayer, exhale thanks

Inhale, exhale softly measure, muffled drum

Taste with once radiation burned buds flaming juices, pomegranate, beet, celery, pulp

Rushing russets

Not easily cracked, somewhat stony, angrily cautious

Like unscored quartz

Mouse, I said, poking nose, is it safe, clear, dangerous place

Holocaust survivors, the violated, flayed

Skinless nerve afraid to leap

Love dark rain-stained dirt

Oh God, just this once, forever penitent or flush me into septic

Walk him out rubble uncrushed

Expel him from tower dust cloud

Deliver from crash

Get him out of there, genitals, head, one piece as born

Damn You

Fucking damn You

Your impenetrability

I demand, bring whole him out that sterilizing psychopathological hell

I love dog, think on that
I love skin, think on that
I love fingernail moon, think on that
I love spume, think on that
I love cello, think
I love sea grass, goat flower, sun lily, polar cup, custard myrtle, candy rocket,
Beverly pop-up, fox vertebra, not-so-pretty, Max's cosmos, donkey's hat, David's
  five-spot, pheasant flax, think on that
I love wheat skate, wheeling Wendy, rake tailed kite, American white rail, Cleopatra
  scaup, ashy dappled thrasher, Swanson's peewit, quartz-throated shearwalker, tra-
  la-la loon, magnificent pugnacious least, bronze-crested crow fish, on that think
I love red dwarf, consider that
I love fontanelle, consider that
I love animadversion, atavism, antimacassar, preternatural, coruscation, uxorious,
  think on that
In God's hands
Child of star breather
Bread of life
Wings like osprey
God equips
One footprint in sand
Oh God, you carry me like meat cape—head slung, hair stuck, lips hung, shoes
  torn, castaway—back to lungful elastic ship on ribcage cove
Oh God, surefooted rock, eagle wing, lighthouse, enough
All in your hands
Please God, kill-shot, says hunter
God, Goal! says center
Sweet magnanimous God, intercourse, says seducer
Fame, says glitterati
Powder, pipeline, trade winds, glass, says sportsmen
Make it swift, says condemned
Enter joke, says comedian
And God jumped hurdles on horse named Never
Rode away, rode away into buttersmoke copse
Which swished closed behind like smoke
Leaving believers shocked, dismayed, angry, dumbfounded.

2.

God leaps off train, thuds, grunts,
Rolls to stop, dusts pants,
Gathers porkpie, dashes for brake
Before discovered, hunted,
scythed by bullets.
Pumped with adrenalin, ravenous,
Terrified of army, townsfolk alike.
Vice crushing lungs breathless.
I'm God he cries, invincible, immortal
But knows he's venous gut sack
Easily eviscerated. Hunger
Forces God into open,
Penniless bum attracting toughs.
Identifies hamlet
On outskirts,
Steals in, pilfers tuber, bloodroot, seed bread,
Good cache for fugitive,
Melts into woods,
Requires inconspicuous duds.
Rags so tattered even clot
Of adolescents, indoctrinated, might murder
Bringing home penis, pinkie
trophy for authorial accolade—
Truancy at circus free of arithmetic.
Suddenly dog growls, snarls, from periphery
Emerges man, boy hitching pants, wielding bats.
Instantaneous recognition of ogre triggers reflex,
Man pummels God's trunk,
Boy stoves God's skull
Spilling brain's raspberry jam,
Mangle body to hairy pulp,
And discover God is female
With rippled cunt which they
Extricate, stick-mount
Like dead chipmunk.
God knew when jumping,
Tattooed for extermination,
Her chances remote.
World knows she releases lice
And cloud of acolytes

Scheduled for liquidation by the pure.
It's simple.
Life's wonderful without plague
So incinerate her
And commemorate the day.

3.

Like blood under ripped off nail
Spirituality pools in brutal fantasies

Anger turned inward as suicide encounters
God rising through entrails

Within rage toward one's mediocrity
Blossoms geranium's rapture

Tranquility fills with agnosticism
Like lovemaking on anesthesia

Shot through terrifying interiors
God's rhythmical stasis of grace

4.

God, stay hand,
Stop beatings,
Banish his fury
Or eliminate him

Swear to God
If betrays
Me again
She's history

God, take my
Life—accident, murder,
Anything—
For his

Not her, God,
Colossal
Error, it
Cant' be so

Strengthen, rip
Me so I can
Jerk myself
From bed

Go with our
Little heroes as
They spill
Onto gridiron

Wave tumbling, lung
Bursting, where is
Up? God deliver
The surface

Pull mattress over
Self in tub,
Ride it out,
Pray to God

God mutilate
Fat fucker
For bullying
My son

Extinguish his soul's
Hellish Torment
In my love

Omnibenevolent God
Magnanimous God
Compassionate God
Forgiving God

I am God. You
Who pray for
Interdiction, I see
Your suffering and
Am implacable..

5.

Brusha brusha brusha. Here's the new Ipana
With a brand new flavor, it's dandy for your te-e-e -th
Sings God.

From the land of sky blue waters, from the land
Of pines, lofty balsams, comes the beer refreshing
Hamm's the beer refreshing, chants God

We're happy little Vegamites, as bright as bright
Can be, we all enjoy our Vegamite, for breakfast,
Lunch, and tea, chirps God

VD—is for everybody, not just the few, anyone
Can share VD with someone nice as you, God intones

Because even an airline hostess should
Look like a girl, chop-licks Lord

Lord says ask, receive
Lord says come unto me
Lord says trust in
Lord says fear no
Lord says abide, igneous
Lord says lamb's blood
Lords says seed into ground, righteous fruits abound
Lord says do not fear, I am near,
        do not be afraid nor dismayed
Lord says, Behold Me risen lamb
        The great unchangeable I AM
Lord says, No matter what may be your test
        Lean weary on My breast
Lord says, I Emmanuel have come to pop Satan's tyranny from sunny heights I
shine, rejoice rejoice in me
What happens next is unbelievable:
Brilliant up-swooshing light like firebird,
Pulsating color-streaked breast,
Some wind-lifted cinematic sylph
Flicking liquid fire,
But that is not it:
Filthy crack-lipped derelict, paranoic

Lousy-bearded, bee-clouded
Rhino feet, rises
Off street, mutters
Invective, slinks
Into universe.
But that is not it:
Sporting charcoal herringbone
Jacket, maroon knit tie,
Having finished Moo Shu Chicken,
Coke, cool professional male
Glides down Enterprise Avenue
Toward nation state
Which he serves.

6.

Numbers crowd brain, random,
Compulsive, objectless:
2-6-7-4-9-7-3-8-8-8-8-8. I count
Stairs as I mount them: 1-2-3-4-5-6-7-8-9-10-11-12-13,
Pivot left, pivot left, 1-2-3-4-5 steps to bed.
Time, too: Four minutes, 9 seconds
409 cubic inch Impala. I count
To 20, all evens, all odds
In blocks of five:
1-3-5-7-9
2-4-6-8-10
11-13-15-17-19
12-14-16-18-20
Rock songs earworm brain,
Wooden Ships,
Voodoo Chile
Like trapped bird flapping walls.
And scrupulosity:
I guilt, I shame, I stain, I shit
Body, soul,
God, char, cut, flay
This worthless sinner's flesh
Please God
Hammer spine with thy fist
Eviscerate inner filth
With instantaneous slash
Savior, Captain, King, Executioner
My Irreproachable Annihilator
Heal with Thy Severity
My rampant brain.
At 50mm rapidity
For reunification
I am prayed and prayed and prayed
Like a madman's marionette.

7.

Take flying leap.
Fly kite.
Long walk, short pier.
Bug off.
And I, spiritual anarchist, waltz across field
Chopped free from loyalties
Bleating in tongues
Like un-penned pig
Dashing for ecstasy
Toward wild horizon—
Fornication, gluttony, idolatry, greed
"God is dead!" "God is nothing!" "Nihilism is king!"
"Long live depravity!"
Sex clubs, pornography, sadism, cruelty
Laced with compassionate loving-kindness
In sardonic contradiction, stuffing gut with pulp
And Hostess custard.
Go boil head
Jump in lake
And I am off into sadistic creativity
Cathartic denouncements
Wiping eyes with Windex
Of irresponsibility.
Hymnal pages as toilet paper.
Unlocked by revelation,
Opened by catharsis,
Freedom bursts through
Amok ideologies
Infinite possibilities
The liberation of creativity
Declaring, like open-winged iron eagle,
Madness sane
Crudity sublime
Profane sacred
Impotence insemination
Godlessness God
In an orgiastically celebrated new world order.

8.

"But that is not what I meant, at all; that is not it, at all."

I click head into shoulders, that magnificent mysterious
machine—psilocybin trip— lasers to perception: skin's
millimeter honeycomb, blood's magnesium river, leaf's
highway system , twig-crack percussion. Excruciating
receptor, I. Brain powers on like surgical eye, chandelier
city, sparkling air, fine wrist hair, rushing atomic cos-
mos, star paint-smear, fathomless black interstices. I
pry open chest, heartbreak rushes out, ecstasy streams in.

"Perhaps that is it, after all; perhaps after all that is it."

Throw switch, world hurts pupils like sizzling tungsten
fuse: productivity, industry, intimacy blindingly
bright: exhaustion, hunger, weakness, clouded
dream—simple historical statistic in misshapen coat,
threadbare dress, mangy cur squatting in mist.
Snapped on sphere crushes one to periphery:
silvery gray wisps, ruins of last year's decomposed
Spring, the infinite natural hues of sand swirls
through, the un-cynical reliable facticity of it.

Death, too, with affixed head, knows God, the
alcohol clear bubble of it, scraped clean crusty
world of it: silver set, maple chest, ruby brooch,
heated seat, mother, child, friend, Wellingtons,
kit and caboodle. Nothingness flooding no-
thingness, finally defined by what was always
there: void, space, ether, antimatter, the abyss
enveloping earthly malodorous rippling grandiosity:
gloss, sheen, bluster, spiff, and the rampant lie.

9.

I suddenly realize I am of the tormented
class. I peel brain to ganglia glow. Only
atheists peel thusly, pores gaping in harsh
stage beam, oily hair, drum roll as infidel
shakes scrotum, mams—lust, gluttony,
sloth, greed—reprobation—are my show
for the whore-shoppers, the Godly ones,
who cherish a good dissolution. I should
have stripped in Berlin cabaret, given it
to fascists at 3AM against wet brick
wall, devoid of rectitude—heretic, lacquered
toes jammed in straps. Let there be
for bloodthirsty acolyte slimy game show
host, all disingenuousness, tacky yellow
tie, "Ugly Edna said," he publicly strips,
"I'm in a tizzy. At airport today as I
went to board the plane, you'll never
guess what happened? My BLANK got
caught in the propeller." There's apostasy
at pole with feather boa. I should have
been, declared famous apostate, pair of
ragged claws scuttling across floor of
silent seas. Oh, please! All you've got?
Crustacean metaphor? Milquetoast! Candy-
ass! You fantasize fornication, throat-
slash, deicide, havoc while prattling
about clacking crab. Suddenly, I realize
I'm one of those…God refusal craters
man to twirl lariat to ratty band on
filthy stage for lecherous drool, baring
engorged scarlet folds or spongy hose
in nihilistic spasm of indomitable sin.

10.

Please God, happiness
Dear God, reprieve
Benevolent God, pleasantry
Give weightlessness, monarch on nose
Bestow love
Confer praise
I am foot soldier firing your rifle of clover, rain
I am acolyte
Please omniscient beatific King proclaim my name to cocksure, loudmouth,
peacock, big shot
Refulgent Lord suffuse vision
I open to You on celestial bed, receptacle of sacred sperm
God Father, God Holy Ghost, God Patriarch imbue me with Lanolin, emollient of
stars
No lackadaisical rower of skiff, I am two-fifty horsepower outboard Yamaha beating
your wake-name: God absolute! God supreme! God incarnate! God side of beef!
So cover me, dear One, with crape, ticker tape, your contemporary Lindberg
landed in Skull after trans-spiritual flight from apostasy to faith
I love frog, I love tamarin, I love colugo, I love pika, I love jaguar, I love kinkajou,
I love duiker, I love okapi; I love catnip, tansy, rue; I love bentbill, pochard, coot; I
love botfly, dragon, wasp; I love all beings, creatures, roots
I am your Havana man, agent provocateur, plain clothes operative in heathen
mistake
Piece of me dies with every demise—murdered, mangled, stillborn, plague
stricken, buried by mud-tongue, stampeded, beaten
Piece of me breathes with every survival
Do not denigrate my lack of cynicism
Academician-derision
I cry spontaneously, driving, walking, stirring pot
God gob stopper
God luge pilot
God fig filling
(Do you think I am kidding
Do you think this is joke
Do you think I care about corporate poetry or establishment fame
This is no poem
Poetry is written by mummies and is dead.)
I have impulse toward violence, control.
To stand on death's neck
To devour and howl
And pleasure pierce my species
And to receive, therefore, through a filthy body, God.

LXXXIII.

I unwrap Santa's gift to me:
church inside box complete
with parishioners, gray heads
and heads past gray to
baking powder white. I am
thrilled. I lift from pulpit—
King Kong—plastic pastor,
mouth open in mid-
benediction, surplice spread
like heron wing. Roof
with New England steeple
snaps off. In vestibule,
miniature tray of cookies.
Toy maker slashed women's
lips red, glossed men's
nails. One congregant looks
stricken—money, illness?
Another absently fidgeting
appears bored, hungry. A
third, transported beyond
material into ether exudes
euphoria. There are no children.